《《 》》

The Predicament
of Modern Man

《《 》》

The Predicament of Modern Man

《《《《   》》》》

By D. ELTON TRUEBLOOD

Author of
The Essence of Spiritual Religion
The Logic of Belief, etc.

Publishers
HARPER & BROTHERS
New York and London

Contents

Preface

A BOOK about a great subject should be either very long or very short, long enough to cover the subject adequately or short enough to permit the presentation of the main line of argument without cluttering detail. Usually both the long book and the short book are needed, but the short book is needed first.

The present volume is the outcome of the conviction that most of our talk about post-war reconstruction misses the point in that the treaties, political organizations, and economic arrangements, about which we speak and write so voluminously, are only surface phenomena. Before any of these can succeed there must be fundamental changes in the foundations of our civilization. It is the conviction of the author that the trouble we face is more profound than we normally suppose and that the solution of our difficulties will likewise lie along deeper lines than we normally suppose. There is nothing more needful at this time than the exploration, by as many minds as possible, of the conditions of the reconstruction of civilization. Since it is civilization itself that is in jeopardy, we must consider, as carefully as we can, what the necessary conditions and presuppositions of any genuine civilization really are.

Any reasonably alert person is aware that there is no single solution to the world's ills now or at any time. The problems before modern man are so complex that neither any single solution nor all solutions put together will give us a really decent world. We do not expect Utopia. A thousand years from now our descendants will be facing difficult times, some of their problems being new and others being the same old problems that plague us today, because they will share inevitably in the perennial human predicament. But we are foolish indeed if we permit a recognition of these limitations on our efforts to dissuade us from effort. To say that no one solution is a panacea is not to deny that some approaches to a problem come nearer to the center of the difficulty than others do. To say that we shall not make a perfect society in the next century or the next millennium is no excuse for failure to do our best to create an order relatively better than the one in which we now live.

One of the heartening facts of our day is the emergence of a philosophy of civilization about which there is great and significant agreement among many who are willing to engage in the intellectual labor which such an inquiry demands. This book is an effort to report faithfully this emerging philosophy, to which many are led who are more concerned with the problems at the center than they are with those at the periphery. Consequently, the function of the author has been the relatively humble one of a clerk of a Friends' meeting who seeks to state faithfully what the "sense of the meeting" is.

D. E. T.

Stanford University,
Lincoln's Birthday, 1944

«« »»

The Predicament
of Modern Man

«« »»

CHAPTER I

The Sickness of Civilization

~~~~~~

We are living today under the sign of the collapse of civilization. The situation has not been produced by the war; the
latter is only a manifestation of it.

<div align="right">ALBERT SCHWEITZER</div>

«««« »»»»

IN THE year 410 A.D. Alaric and his Goths
sacked the city of Rome. This event was of vast
importance in the ancient world, not so much because of its direct effect on political or economic
organization, but because of its effect on the minds
of men and women who shared in the Mediterranean civilization. The sack was not the most terrible
of visitations, but it was a profound shock, and it
was likewise a revelation. For centuries men had
thought of Rome as a stable feature of civilized
existence. She had been intact from the invader for
nearly a thousand years. Provinces might revolt
and provinces might be pacified, but Rome was the
Eternal City. She was the assurance of order, and
men had come to believe, without argument, in the
dependability of that order. But the shock of invasion revealed to men throughout the Mediterranean
theater the inadequacy of that on which they had

depended with such implicit faith. The consequence was that they were forced to question the entire civilization on which they had relied. We see evidence of the enduring effect of this shock throughout the structure of St. Augustine's great work, *The City of God*, which was not finished until sixteen years after the event that precipitated its writing. The whole book is a monumental attempt to speak to the condition of men and women suffering from a profound intellectual and spiritual shock. Augustine's arguments show clearly the questionings and probings in men's minds. They all recognized that the trouble was more than superficial and that 410 represented more than an isolated military defeat. The fall of Rome was, not the *cause* of the decay of their culture, but rather a *symptom* of that decay. The decay, they realized, must have been much further advanced than was generally recognized.

What was the cause of the decay? Did it come, as some supposed, from disloyalty to their old pagan faiths, or were there other and far different reasons for failure? What could events teach them concerning the foundations on which civilization might be rebuilt?

We have now a counterpart of the ancient situation. *Much as men lived for years under the shadow of 410, we shall live for years under the shadow of 1940.* The chief problems we face are not the problems of the war, great as these are. If they were, they would end when the war ends, but they go too deep for that. The shadow of 1940 will not be removed by the technical conclusion of military hostilities nor by the organization of a peace conference. This is because the war is only a symptom of the sickness of our civilization and not the primary cause of that sickness.

The vast importance of 1940 in our time lies in the fact that the weakness of an entire system in which we had great faith was then revealed to civilized mankind. The fall of France, though only one item in this historical situation, has been the most striking and the most shocking. France was a symbol of an entire kind of life that we had come to take for granted in the Western world. It represented the *urbanity*, the *individualism*, the *humaneness*, the *intelligence* that we had come to prize. Frenchmen were internationally minded, Frenchmen were relatively free from race prejudice, Frenchmen were thrifty, Frenchmen believed in freedom of speech, freedom of thought, and freedom of worship. Here, it seemed, was the quintessence of Western civilization, which we had taken for centuries as our standard of comparison, and suddenly we realized that the new Rome was no more a match for the barbarian than the ancient Rome had been. In short it was demonstrated, in such a manner that all could see, that Western civilization lacked the security which we, in our innocence, had attributed to it.

The spiritual crisis engendered by this shock could by no means be limited to Europe, but was bound to affect the entire life of man on the planet. In the fall of Rome it was chiefly Mediterranean civilization that was at stake, while other areas of the globe were largely unaffected. The civilization of Christendom, on the other hand, has so penetrated all parts of the world that all are affected by what happens to us.

The civilization of the West, that is to say, the Christian civilization, is only one of several concurrent civilizations. It is a mistake to regard our society as identical with civilized mankind and all others as "natives" of territories that they inhabit by sufferance.[1] The white man's burden is not that heavy. But, though our civilization is only one civilization among others, the relationships between civilizations is now such that our civilization involves all others in its own predicament. There are two major reasons for this. First, the development of modern technology is such that all parts of the planet are close to all other parts in time and in the consequent impossibility of isolation. In the words of Mr. Willkie's inspired title, ours is really *One World* in the technical sense. Any new flood is bound to cover the entire earth.

The second reason for the inclusion of all in our predicament is the fact that Christian culture has

[1] See Arnold Toynbee, *A Study of History*, Vol. I, p. 33. Toynbee holds that there are at least four other living societies of the same species as ours.

penetrated other cultures much more than they have penetrated ours. Western man has penetrated all parts of the globe educationally, industrially, and religiously. Our predicament is not a local matter, but a matter of planetary concern because Western man, partly through his aggressiveness, though chiefly through his technical prowess, is the dominant man on the planet.[2] The predicament, therefore, is not merely the predicament of *Western* man, but of *man*.

The recognition that something has gone wrong with our civilization is now so widespread as to be almost universal. Much of this has arisen from the obvious discrepancy between the promises and the achievements of our age. There is no doubt that faith in a more or less automatic progress was widespread a generation ago, when it was assumed that the fruits of our cleverness would be good fruits. The increase of science, many supposed, would ensure a brave new world. Science was to unify the world (which it has) and bring in a day of universal brotherhood (which it has not). Characteristic of this pathetic faith is the following conclusion of F. S. Marvin, whose words were widely read twenty years ago:

And now, of all consolidators, science is showing its supreme fitness and its kinship with the sense of

[2] The fact that this dominance is now being challenged does not alter the truth of this observation. It is the titleholder who is challenged.

a common humanity. It would be a fascinating and untrodden path, to follow in the ancient world the extension of scientific knowledge and note its coincidence with the growth of a more humane spirit in religion, in poetry, and in law. We believe the agreement would be close and that it is more than a mere coincidence. But here the evidence would be slighter and less conclusive: in the modern world the case is clear. Side by side with the growth of science, which is also the basis of the material prosperity and unification of the world, has come a steady deepening of human sympathy, and the extension of it to all weak and suffering things. . . . Science, founding a firmer basis for the co-operation of mankind, goes widening down the centuries, and sympathy and pity bind the courses together.[3]

This hope, by no means rare, is now seen to be utterly unjustified. At the precise time when our vaunted education comes to mature development we see all about us the outbreak of man's inhumanity to man in such fashion that our faith is shaken. We are not so gullible as we were. How can we be so sure that Western civilization is really better than any of its alternatives, if we are to judge it by its fruits after years of opportunity? After all, the epidemic has broken out, not in some primitive area, but in the supposed heart of Christendom.

This seems to be the chief ground of the often-mentioned lack of enthusiasm on the part of our people. Whereas the Germans, especially the youth, have entered the conflict with fanatical zeal, comparable with that of those who extended Islam with

[3] F. S. Marvin, *The Living Past*, Oxford, 1923, pp. 270, 271.

the sword, our people are extremely shy about any emotional appeal. The Axis propagandists are able to arouse their countries to a furious crusade, but the few who try to arouse us in a similar way are met with a quizzical look. The band-playing hilarity of leave-takings, which the fathers knew, is quite unknown to the sons. For the most part the struggle goes on as a sober, hateful business, with little romance and with few illusions. It may be that we are too dull and businesslike today, but at least we are safe from the kind of disillusionment that occurred so disastrously before, when romantic idealism was followed by general cynicism. If we experience a revolt this time, it will have to be a revolt in the other direction.

We cannot, of course, expect so much suffering without the emergence of skepticism, but the skepticism of one period is not the same as the skepticism of another. The mood in which we find ourselves may be accurately termed the "New Skepticism." Those to whom men turned for spiritual counsel in the earlier struggle were forced to deal with skepticism about God. "Why," men asked repeatedly, "would God allow this terrible calamity? Why does God permit His children to destroy each other?" Today, however, this inquiry is seldom heard. In place of it there has come another kind of inquiry, which represents a deep skepticism about mankind. Instead of asking, "Why does God allow it?" thousands now ask, "How could man have made such a mess of things?"

The change in popular sentiment is great though not sufficient. The chief ways in which this change appears are the rejection of the belief in the essential goodness of man and the twin belief in automatic progress. We have not arrived at a sufficient substitute, but in any case we have escaped from the chief dangers of optimism.

It is hard to tell how much of the present skepticism about the worth of our human civilization has come as a result of revealing experience and how much has come as a result of published thought on the subject. In any case it is true that many thoughtful people had already arrived at grave doubts about the true value of our boasted culture when the great majority appeared to have no doubts at all. Now the public has caught up with the prophets, so far as their pessimism is concerned.

The men who began to challenge the sense of security of our age arrived at their conclusions on various grounds. Thus Henry Adams, believing in the universal applicability of the second law of thermodynamics, predicted necessary cultural decline in *The Degradation of Democratic Dogma*, while Spengler espoused a theory of cycles that was neither democratic nor Christian. Later there appeared several independent thinkers who began to reveal the sickness of our civilization in the light of Christian theology.

Twenty-one years ago Albert Schweitzer said, "It is clear now to everyone that the suicide of civilization is in progress. What yet remains of it is no longer safe. It is still standing, indeed, because it was not exposed to the destructive pressures which overwhelmed the rest, but, like the rest, it built upon rubble, and the next landslide will very likely carry it away."[4] Of course, this was *not* clear to everyone. The amazing thing is that it was already clear to this lonely man, living, not in Europe, but on the edge of the African jungle. Many of his contemporaries were wholly convinced that man had come into a new time, a time of general prosperity and of happiness through abundance. One hot night that summer President Harding died in San Francisco, and Calvin Coolidge became head of the nation. With him came added prosperity, and who then cared about a philosophical doctor in Africa?

Nikolai Berdyaev was already expressing, at the same time, a similar skepticism. His book, *The End of Our Time*, was written when most people appeared to think we were both safe and sound. Spengler's *Decline of the West* had been taken seriously by a few, but not by the masses. The surprising fact is that so many prophets saw the weakness of our civilization when it seemed strongest.

[4] Albert Schweitzer, *The Decay and Restoration of Civilization*, London, 1923, p. 3.

Just as we were ridding the world of Kaiser and Czar, Spengler predicted the rise of Caesarism. The prophets, writing in 1922 and 1923, sensed that the Armistice was only an armistice. The uniting conviction of a number of advanced theologians was the notion that the war was really a revelation. It revealed, said Berdyaev, "the superficiality of the process of humanization and how thin was the layer of human society which had really been affected by the humanizing forces."[5]

An important fact, which we do not sufficiently realize, is that Adolf Hitler was one of these prophets writing two decades ago. His conclusions were poles apart from those of Schweitzer and Berdyaev, but he was in full agreement with these men about the decay of the received culture. His error, as we see it now, lay not in his quick perception of a profound trouble, but in the false simplicity of his diagnosis of causes and in his prescribed cure, which did so much to heighten the existing fever. He knew that the breakdown of a world view was far more important than the breakdown of an economic or political structure and that we must go beyond the outward sickness to the inner causes. "All those symptoms of decay," wrote Hitler in 1924, "are in the last analysis only the consequences of the absence of a definite, uniformly acknowledged philosophy and the resultant general uncer-

[5] Nikolai Berdyaev, *The Fate of Man in the Modern World*, p. 9.

tainty in the judgment and attitude toward the various great problems of the time." The defeat of Germany, he maintained was not an isolated catastrophe, but wholly reasonable and wholly deserved. "It is only the greatest outward symptom of decay amid a whole series of inner symptoms, which perhaps had remained hidden and invisible to the eyes of most people, or which like ostriches people did not want to see."[6]

The point is that the world has now caught up with Hitler and Berdyaev and Schweitzer. We now know that the disease of Western civilization was much further advanced than it appeared to be when attention was paid to superficial symptoms. It took a prophet to know that the First World War was a revelation instead of a mere war, but the common citizen knows that the present struggle is far more than a war. The old fashioned "war" now seems a relatively decent affair, in which most of those who were killed were in the army and in which psychological warfare was not the dominant phase. If there had been no "war," i.e., if the Munich idea had succeeded and Hitler had been able to pose as a man of "peace," there would be just as many symptoms of the fundamental sickness as there are now. Perhaps there would be more!

The sickness is all one sickness, but it was at a far more advanced stage in 1939 than it was in

[6] Adolf Hitler, *Mein Kampf*, translated by Ralph Manheim, Boston, Houghton Mifflin Company, 1943, pp. 266, 229, 230.

1914. Indeed, the sickness was so much further advanced that it produced radically new symptoms or old symptoms so altered and so heightened that they appeared in new ways. All through the autumn of 1938 we tried to persuade ourselves that the disease was not so bad as it seemed. After the Ides of March, 1939, we knew just how serious the malady was, and there has been little doubt since.[7] Man's life on this planet has never been a bed of roses, and a certain amount of physical suffering we naturally expect, but a great part of the suffering of our time is of the mind. The worst ravages have not happened to men's houses or even to their bodies. There is no record in history of such widespread violence and anxiety as mark our time.

The emphasis on the sickness is very important because only through accurate diagnosis is there a chance of successful recovery. For one thing, the recognition that we are enduring more than a war keeps us from dividing the world neatly into two camps, ourselves and our enemies. We are not free from the basic trouble ourselves. If what we had on our hands were merely a war, we might expect to have a reasonably secure future, by means of treaties and the like, if and when we gain the victory.

[7] The author was in England during the critical days of 1939 and was able to note the great change in public opinion that came with the open violation of the Munich Agreement on March 15. For many the strain was gone. At last they knew how serious the situation was and how long the road to peace might be.

But treaties are superficial remedies indeed when the trouble is as deep as ours now is. Neither political nor economic re-arrangements will suffice. Just as the difficulty lies deeper than we at first supposed, so the path of recovery will lie along deeper lines than we have realized.

It is obvious that there must be a peculiar combination of factors which have produced the present crisis. We cannot account for the present series of calamities merely by reference to the natural depravity of the human heart, however great it may be, for that is presumably a constant factor and there are aspects of the present situation which are by no means constant. Since the phase of man's life which makes modern man's situation most obviously different from that of all his ancestors is technical or mechanical achievement, it is reasonable to suspect that our predicament is associated, in some way or other, with this development.

The human crisis involves a combination of factors that is paradoxical in the extreme, and much of the paradox lies in the relationship between the means and ends of our culture. The *means* of our culture, i.e., our *technics*, are developed wonderfully by rational experimental and precise thought, but the ends have not kept pace. The technical progress, though it makes for dehumanization, involves the great hope of universalism, since it provides the means of making mankind physically *one*.

It is our technical progress that now brings any one spot on the globe within a few hours' travel of every other spot, which makes it possible to send messages to all the earth at once and which makes no spot safe or secure against aggression.

The awful truth is that our wisdom about ends does not match our ingenuity about means, and this situation, if it continues, may be sufficient to destroy us. Just at the moment of history when the technical conditions for the oneness of the globe have finally appeared, we are woefully lacking in the moral conditions that are required if this situation is to be a blessing. It is not merely that this contrast removes us from a fortunate situation; *it actually produces a situation far more evil than any formerly known. Because of lack of moral direction, what might have been a blessing becomes a terrible curse.*

The moral failure to match the technical achievement is seen in three different ways in three different groups. It is seen first in Japan, a country that has taken over the instruments of Christendom without the moral and religious principles of Christendom. It is seen second in Germany, and to some extent in Russia, where the moral and religious conceptions of Christendom have been deliberately rejected, after having long been known. It is seen, in the third place, in the Western democracies, where we still pay lip service to the moral and religious principles of Christendom but have actually lost a great part of this heritage.

The gravity of our situation in regard to means and ends becomes clearer when we realize that the present combination of means and ends is the worst of all possible combinations. The contemporary contrast in the relative development of engineering and ethics is the most dangerous that could be. If we have regard to the factors unifying or dividing mankind, there are four possible combinations, as follows:

(1) *Divisive purposes served by inadequate instruments*. This, we suppose, was the situation throughout most of human pre-history and much of human history. The leaders of the clan may seek the destruction or harm of all outside the clan, but the tools available are such that these purposes remain unaccomplished for the most part.

(2) *Unifying purpose served by inadequate instruments*. This has been the situation of most of the dreamers of world brotherhood. Their desire for the general welfare of mankind has been baffled, not only by the opposite desires of their contemporaries, but also by the lack of technical ability to accomplish desired ends.

(3) *Divisive purposes served by potent instruments*, i.e., *universalizing instruments*. This is the actual situation in many parts of the present world and the potential situation everywhere. The possible blight which might come to the human spirit if a minority of wholly ruthless men should achieve a monopoly on the instruments of power that make

the world all one province, technically, is a reasonable cause for fear.

(4) *Unifying purposes served by potent instruments.* This situation, which has never yet appeared in any large way, would be the most conducive to the flowering of the human spirit that we can imagine. If our ends sought were as rational and as catholic as our technology is, man would still have his evil impulses but the world would be such that most of us would be glad for the chance to live in it. It is the situation we earnestly seek.

We are now in the tragic third possibility inasmuch as man has been more successful in making engines than in achieving the will and wisdom to use his engines for humane purposes. This is the predicament of Western man. He has built up a complex civilization, but he may lose it because, in his proud hour of achievement, he has so largely lost or never developed the inner resources that are needed to keep a possible boon from becoming a calamity.

It is important to make it abundantly clear at this point that the crucial problem is the spiritual problem, and we here mean by spiritual that area which is the object of attention in philosophy and theology as against that area in which the object of attention is mechanical contrivance. The fact that our life is so gravely threatened in the brightest day of technical achievement is not a criticism of the engineers *qua* engineers, but it is a criticism of all of us as *men*. The paradox of failure at the moment of success is by no means a condemnation of technical progress, for such progress is morally neutral. It gives the surgeon's knife, and it gives the gangster's weapon. Our predicament is a commentary, not on instruments and instrument makers, but on the human inability to employ both scientific knowledge and technical achievement to bring about the good life and the good society. Man is an animal who is peculiarly in need of something to buttress and to guide his spiritual life. Without this, the very capacities that make him a little lower than the angels lead to his destruction. The beasts do not need a philosophy or a religion, but man does.

When we say that the most urgent problem of our time is the spiritual problem we are opposing directly the popular opinion. *Most people do not believe it*. It is curious to note the way in which our world calamity has destroyed some of our comfortable delusions, but not others. Thus we have been pretty well emancipated from the dogma of automatic progress and even from faith in the goodness of man. In these matters we have shown some ability to be taught by experience. But we have not been equally emancipated from the belief that economic and technical reconstruction are enough. We suppose, quite naïvely, that the problem of spiritual reconstruction will take care of itself or that it can be left to the experts as a departmental matter.

The lesson of our time is that this delusion is no better than any other delusion. The problem will *not* take care of itself. Unless the spiritual problem is solved, civilization will fail; indeed, we already have a foretaste of that failure in many parts of the world. Man's sinful nature is such that he will use instruments of power for evil ends unless there is something to instruct him in their beneficent uses. Without the conscious and intelligent buttressing of what has been demonstrated as precious, human society goes down.

It ought to be clear to us that such a task is so amazingly difficult that we should employ our greatest single effort in this direction. If we had even the beginning of wisdom, we should encourage our brightest men and women to devote themselves to the task of spiritual reconstruction. We should put our best thought into the elaboration and promulgation of an adequate faith rather than into some new machine.

How far we are from doing this is obvious. In our public schools we teach our children many things about our modern world, such as our system of manufacture and distribution, but we make almost no effort to give them a living knowledge of the spiritual sources of our civilization. We deliberately cut them off from their heritage. In America we actually work, in many states, on the preposterous theory that it is illegal to teach our children the faith on which our democracy rests. The public school teacher can tell all she likes about Nero, but she cannot tell about his distinguished contemporary, St. Paul. In any case she cannot tell what the open secret of St. Paul's life was. In most of our universities there are hundreds of young men devoting themselves to careful preparation in engineering or the natural sciences as against one devoting himself to careful preparation in philosophy or theology. A similar unbalance is shown in university curricula and budgetary allotments.

The sober truth is that, as a people, we do not believe we are engaged in a race with catastrophe. We are not aware of the dangers we face, and consequently we are doing relatively little to meet them. If we could put the same keen intelligence and careful judgment into the revival of faith and the discovery of the proper objects of faith that we now put into the production of magnificent machines, man's life on this earth might come into a new and glorious day. We fail to do this because we do not read the signs of the times or listen to our prophets. The situation, which would appear alarming if only men were apprized of it, is stated by one of these prophets as follows:

If you allow the spiritual basis of a civilization to perish, you first change, and finally destroy it. Christianity and Hellenism are the spiritual bases of our civilization. They are far less powerful today than fifty years ago. Therefore, we are losing that spiritual basis, and our civilization is changing and on the way to destruction, unless we can reverse the process.[8]

"Unless we can reverse the process"—there is the heart of the problem. Perhaps we cannot do so; perhaps we are dealing with a wave of the future or a renewed wave of the past that is already bearing us forward in frightening or eventually heartening ways. But until we know this is the case, our task is to make every effort to build our society as free men.

The two most striking examples of how human life may be guided, so far as our tradition is concerned, are seen in Greek philosophy and the Christian religion. In ancient Greece there was a widespread popular teaching of philosophy, with Cynics, Stoics, and Epicureans preaching a rule of life. Eventually this gave way to the Christian faith, which has been the dominant spiritual force in the West through most of the succeeding centuries. Even fifty years ago, in our English-speaking countries it was still effective. Nearly everyone read the Bible and engaged in public and private prayer, as well as family prayer, and great numbers heard, once each week, sermons that expounded the gospel. Once a week there was a day that reminded all people of a dimension of their lives other than those of the surface.

Now most of this is gone. Philosophy today

[8] Sir Richard Livingstone, *The Future in Education*, Cambridge University Press, 1943, p. 113.

touches only a tiny class of people who happen to take courses in universities or read an occasional book. The Christian faith has lost much of its hold. Of course, it is still possible to present impressive census figures showing that the number of church members in this country is the largest in relation to the total population that it has ever been,[9] but these figures are not convincing. Nearly all the membership rolls are padded, since, in many churches, all baptized persons are included in membership. Everyone knows that great numbers of these are totally dissociated from the influences of public worship.

The signs of the decay of the Christian faith are so great on every side that only wishful thinking can deny it. Convenient illustrations are the contemporary ignorance of the Bible, the decline of the observance of a day of worship, and the loosening of the marriage tie. It is possible that Christianity is now lingering very much as paganism lingered on into the Christian era. Those men in Rome who supposed their woes came from disloyalty to the pagan gods were fighting a hopeless battle, and the same may be true of the contemporary apologist for the Christian faith.

We continue to call our era the Christian Era, but this may be for no better reason than the difficulty of changing a frame of temporal reference

[9] There are now 67,327,719 church members in the United States of America according to the *Yearbook of the Churches.*

when it has once been established all over the world. Mussolini's attempt to introduce his own system of dating from the beginning of the Fascist Era, referring to his own definitive speeches of the year Twelve[10] seems to most of us merely ridiculous, but he might be nearer right than we think. *The truth is that we still have not decided which century this is. We do not really know whether it is the twentieth century or the first.* There are few more important questions that man can ask.

Regardless of the personal position he takes, it is not possible for a thoughtful person to view lightly the apparent crumbling of the Christian pattern. Whether for good or ill, such a development is momentous. If Western man, who has long been the dominant man on the planet, should now lose those ultimate convictions which have been partly regulative for at least fifteen centuries, the change would be enormous. Temporarily, at least, the change has already occurred, and this change has been more crucial than any battle or other external event. *It is the chief event that has occurred.* A change in the meaning of truth or of justice is far more important than a change in the government of any given territory. "The Axis powers would not have initiated the crisis in civilization or forced this war on the world if they had not repudiated these values in advance."[11]

[10] Benito Mussolini, *The Corporate State*, Florence, 1938, XVI, p. 62.
[11] H. G. Wood, *Christianity and Civilization*, p. 5.

The greatness of the possible change becomes clear when we realize the degree to which the civilization of the West has been the civilization of Christendom. It is far more Christian than Greek or Roman, since classic culture contributed to modern culture, not *directly*, but only as assimilated by Christianity. The late Professor Bosanquet, who had drunk deeply from classic sources, saw this so clearly and expressed it so tersely that his dictum is here repeated: "Christianity is the form in which the progressive civilization of Greece and Rome expressed its tendencies when time and experience had partly matured them."[12] Greece and Rome did not survive as cultural entities; instead, they contributed to that which did survive; and that which did survive is Christianity.

The magnitude of our possible revolution becomes clearer when we think of the degree to which the gospel has permeated the unargued groundwork of our culture. This permeation is shown by the reasons people give for what they do and especially in the excuses they give for their moral failures. The ultimate appeal is usually made to the welfare of others rather than to the capricious desire of the person whose actions are under consideration. The ideological leaders of the Fascist and Nazi revolutions have tried to alter this form of ultimate appeal, but even they have had difficulty

[12] Bernard Bosanquet, *The Civilization of Christendom*, London, 1893, p. 75. See also Walter Horton, *Can Christianity Save Civilization?* p. 67 n.

in maintaining a consistent rejection of the ethical presuppositions of Western civilization. Mussolini himself, perhaps in a weak moment, defended the conquest of Ethiopia on grounds that he owed more to the New Testament than to the neo-paganism which he claimed to preach. "Italy," he wrote, "is conquering territory in Africa, but in doing so she is freeing populations who for thousands of years have been at the mercy of a few bloodthirsty and rapacious chieftains."[13] Of course, if he had been consistent, the writer would have extolled the bloodthirstiness and rapacity of these chieftains, seeing in them models of the new and strong morality, but it is hard to be consistent all the time. It is especially hard when one is dealing with fundamental presuppositions that have influenced human judgments for so many centuries.

Now it is these particular presuppositions that are in jeopardy. The West has turned against its own genius. We have seen it break down before our eyes in the huge and terrifying object lesson that Central Europe provides. What frightens all reasonable people is the fact that we see about us, in our own neighborhoods, some of the same factors which, existing in greater degree, made that object lesson actual. How can we keep the evil from spreading? Certainly the mere defeat of the Axis Powers will not be sufficient to prevent this. Our greatest menace is not from *Germany*, great as this

[13] *Op. cit.*, p. 86.

has been, but rather from the same mood that gripped Germany so powerfully and so destructively.

We are superficially safe in the Western democracies so long as the war lasts, but the danger will be enormous when the fighting ends. A host of new problems will arise, bringing new temptations. We must remember that, after the First World War, the epidemic broke out first in Italy and then in Germany because these patients were weaker. The germs are everywhere, *and we shall be weaker later*. Epidemics, like empires, often move West.

Now the problem is this: What is going to buttress our spiritual life in this time of unparalleled danger, when the ancient supports are gone? What are the modern equivalents of the philosophies of the ancient world and the Christian faith of our fathers? Is it the gospel of "freedom" in the sense of rejection of all limitations on private whim? Is it some dark revival of paganism? Is it some general talk about the democratic way of life? These are among the most important questions that a man can ask.

Our problem is not to *save* Western culture, in the sense of merely keeping something from the past. Much of what we have had we do not wish to see restored, because it is bad. What we are concerned with in Western civilization is not its restoration, but the achievement of the promise that has long been implicit within it. In any case, the ideal is clear. What we seek is a situation in which we so combine scientific and technical skill with moral and spiritual discipline that the products of human genius shall be used for the welfare of the human race rather than their harm and destruction.

Since the practical task now is the spiritual task, as we have defined it, we must consider the genuine alternatives before us. These are essentially three, (1) the new gospel of power culture, which rejects our historic faith; (2) some effort to keep the fruits of our culture apart from its religion; or (3) a reaffirmation of the Christian faith. It is conceivable that, apart from such a reaffirmation, there is no possibility of a really civilized life on the global scale that modern conditions require. But this is a question that we must decide on the basis of the available evidence. In the succeeding chapters of this book we shall examine some of the available evidence, beginning with the first major alternative and following the argument wherever it leads.

CHAPTER II

The Failure of Power Culture

Partisan, religious, humanitarian and all other criteria in general, are completely irrelevant.

ADOLPH HITLER

《《《《　》》》》

NOT all who note the sickness of Western civilization are saddened by this. There are some who are glad that it is sick and hope it will die. The sooner it dies the better, they suppose, because they believe the central faith of Western man has been a mistake. This is especially true of those who look upon the Christian religion as an impediment to the full development of a strong, heroic age. With its constant emphasis on a moral imperative it has dampened natural enthusiasms and made man a tame creature. What is desirable, they think, is to set men free from the shackles of the Christian centuries and thus make way for the restoration of the old gusty life in which the strong are able to glory in their strength.

It might be argued that this way should be given a fair trial, inasmuch as the Christian way has already been tried a long time and does not seem to have been a marked success. Why not see what frank neo-paganism would do for the world?

Fortunately, so far as our decision is concerned, the problem is not a purely speculative one, since the suggested basis of culture has already been tried. It has been tried, not only in the ancient world, but in our own twentieth century. We are living in a time that is as exciting as it is sad, because we have seen a laboratory test of the old idea in a new setting. To a degree that would have seemed fantastic in prospect, the Nazi youth have been trained in the entire renunciation of the Christian ethic. It is a controlled experiment. Thousands of young people have been deliberately cut off from the cultural tradition that Western man has known for many centuries; they have been taught either to despise or to ignore the Christian ethic. The experiment has been carried on long enough, over a large enough area, and with sufficient methodological rigor to make it a ground for reasonable conclusions.

The experiment that has been undertaken with conscious deliberation in Germany is an accentuation of what has been happening in lesser degree in the entire Western world. In many areas of the West there has been the tacit rejection of our ancient culture, but without a pagan apologetic. The loosening of the marriage tie is one of the many evidences of this development. There have, of course, always been difficulties about monogamy, but acceptance of the Christian estimate of the sacredness of the marriage tie made men have a bad conscience when marriage failed. Now we have great numbers who appear to be able to contemplate their failure with entire complacency. And the reason is that marriage seems to them, not a sacramental act, but rather a temporary convenience. The Hollywood mentality is, in this regard, merely a grotesque accentuation of the general spirit of the times.

What is so amazing in our day is not the rejection of Western civilization in *practice*, for that has always occurred, but the rejection of Western civilization in *theory*. So long as the theory remains intact, there is always hope of regeneration, since some men will be disturbed by their hypocrisy. But when the theory goes, too, there is no hope; there is nothing to give men a bad conscience. It is bad enough to fail to live up to humane standards, but it is far worse to glory in that failure.

The reconstruction of human history which is presented to us as a live option is so revolutionary that we have had great difficulty in taking it seriously. It is well known that one of the reasons for Hitler's initial and long-continued success is that his propositions seemed so preposterous that even those who stood most chance to be ruined by them refused to take them seriously. We did not understand him at first because we could not grasp the notion that his concept of culture was "non-Euclid-

ean."[1] We could not really believe that here was
a system which introduced, not merely different
conclusions, but different rules and different mean-
ings for major terms. We have been slow to realize
that a generation has now grown up in one part of
the Western world in which terms used for more
than fifteen centuries in Europe now have no meaning at all or vastly altered meaning. Sir Richard
Livingstone has stated this point in words that
should be repeated:

They do not know the meaning of certain words,
which had been assumed to belong to the permanent
vocabulary of mankind, certain ideals which, if ignored
in practice under pressure, were accepted in theory.
The least important of these words is Freedom. The
most important are Justice, Mercy and Truth. In
the past we have slurred this revolution over as a difference in "ideology." In fact it is the greatest trans-
formation that the world has undergone, since, in
Palestine or Greece, these ideas came into being or at
least were recognized as principles of conduct.[2]

This new conception of civilization which pre-
sents itself as an alternative to that which has done
duty so far in Western life in our era must be taken
seriously. Its proponents will be defeated in Germany as they have already been defeated in Italy,
but the idea will not, for that reason, be dead. Not
only will there be the hosts of young people who
have been indoctrinated in the non-Euclidean ethics,

[1] The introduction of this illuminating term in this connection originated, I believe, with Lewis Mumford. See his
Faith for Living, pp. 182 ff.

[2] Sir Richard Livingstone, *The Future in Education*, p. 109.

but there will be the many temptations to introduce similar ideas throughout other parts of the West.

It is convenient to refer to this alternative proposal for the human race as *power culture*. We have long used the term "power politics," and it is reasonable to expand the usage to include the entire cultural situation. The essential notion of power culture is the effort to organize human life independent of moral inhibitions. It is the non-ethical creed.[3] It is the supposition, which Mussolini and his pupils have acted on thoroughly, while the rest of us have acted on it amateurishly, that civilization consists primarily in scientific, technical, and artistic achievements and that it can reach its goal without ethical considerations. We see this more clearly if we note, in some detail, the chief items of this creed.

(1) *The first item in this creed is the accent on sheer power*. The notable fact about human life is that some are strong and others are weak. Consequently the fundamental human relation is that of master and slave. Christianity has been a kill-joy because it has hampered the natural power of the master, which must no longer be hampered. Justice, as Thrasymachus said long ago in *The Republic*, is nothing more or less than the interests of the stronger.

Though this doctrine is a very old one, never

[3] "They carried to the logical limit the new cult of power. In the face of all human experience, they assumed that politics and industry could be completely divorced from morals." Mumford, *op. cit.*, p. 182.

wholly dead, it gains modern significance, when openly espoused, because human power has been so greatly enhanced in our day. Science, indeed, is power. Therefore the proponents of power culture will seek to foster science because science makes the strong man's arm longer and his feet swifter. Apart from the infinitely careful and sometimes painful labor of science we should not have the machine, and the machine is absolutely necessary as a tool for those who wish to make their will felt in the modern world. So great is the power of the machine that it is wholly conceivable that a ruthless minority might inaugurate a reign of terror which would include all parts of the planet. "Technics," says Berdyaev, "rationalize human life, but this rationalization has irrational results."[4]

It is important to note that skill in war, an essential element in the power concept, may be marked while moral sensitivity is weak. There is no guarantee of balanced development in the human animal. An interesting illustration of this unbalance is afforded by the experience of the Aztecs, who, for a while, were able to combine great and ruthless military skill with a decadent general culture. They produced some art, including poetry, but it was of a uniformly morbid character. The appearance of the Aztec type of life on a large scale would be a terrifying prospect.

[4] Nikolai Berdyaev, *The Fate of Man in the Modern World*, p. 73.

(2) *The second item in this creed is the concept of leadership.* The way is made clear for the emergence of this concept when the notion of human equality is categorically denied. Equality is a pure fiction; it does not exist physically, intellectually, morally, or culturally. It is entirely satisfactory that there should be masters and slaves, leaders and led. This is a situation, not to be outgrown, but to be accentuated and maintained.

As usually presented the doctrine has two aspects, one personal and the other racial or national. The personal aspect is the emergence of the single leader, who at once commands his people and becomes identified with them, so that his decisions are somehow theirs.[5] The racial aspect is that one people is superior to all others, just as there are superior horses or cows, and these exemplify the leader principle in the human race as a whole. They must keep themselves pure biologically by refusal to mate with inferior breeds, and they must keep themselves pure spiritually by refusing to accept any inferior status or to grant equality when equality does not exist.

The leader principle thus sets itself in sharp contrast to three fundamental Christian teachings. It renounces, first, the Christian notion of human

[5] Spengler predicted the rise of Caesarism as a national development in our period of declining vigor. See *The Decline of the West*, Vol. II, Chap. XIV. But, long before Spengler, William Penn wrote, "Men must be governed by God or they will be ruled by tyrants."

equality, it renounces, second, the Christian notion of the oneness of the human family, and it renounces, third, the Christian rejection of pride. Christ's words, "Call no man master," are arrant nonsense to one who accepts the leader principle as valid.

(3) *The third item in the creed of power culture is the principle of authority.* This does not mean merely the acceptance of the authority of the expert, without which we could not even live; it goes much further. It means that the ideal organization is that in which the individuals live in unquestioning obedience and glory in doing so. The people, we are told, will be happy because they are set free in a curious manner; they are set free from *freedom.*

This conception is the direct renunciation of two highly prized features of our Western civilization, experimentalism and individualism. The experimental spirit, which takes as its text, "Try all things; hold fast that which is good," has been the source of much that we have prized, especially in science, but it has very little place in power culture. In a wholly authoritarian system the experimenter would not be free to declare his disquieting results. since, if they did not contribute to the success of the race or nation, they would not be "true."

That individualism is incompatible with the proposed creed is easy to see. The notion that each person is a separate object of infinite worth because he is a child of God made in God's image must be rooted out if sheer authoritarianism is to flourish.

Our age, which began as a revolt against authority, became in short order one more addicted to authority than has usually been the case with mankind. When we wish to refer to an authoritarian epoch, it is no longer necessary to find our illustrations in the past. Few events are so instructive in this connection as the quick metamorphosis of the German Youth movement and its incorporation into the Hitler movement. If we understand the reasons for this change from revolt against authority to meek acceptance of authority, we are in a better position to appreciate the dangers in all parts of our Western life. Why cannot similar developments take place elsewhere?

As he faces this daring composite proposal, which amounts to a secession from Christendom with the avowed intention of making the secession movement dominant, the ordinary man is curiously helpless. He does not like Hitler and he does not like Hitler's creed, but he has very little notion of what to do about it. He understands what to do in a military way, but he does not understand what to do in an intellectual way. He mumbles something about democracy, but he seldom examines the moral grounds that make democracy possible, and he has no living faith to put in the place of the heretical one that is so vigorously preached. He will, we agree, win the "war," in the sense that the Nazis will be stripped of their power to hold others in physical slavery and tyranny, but he may, nevertheless, lose the "struggle." The *Kampf* is much broader than the "war."

The chief weakness of modern Western man is weakness of the head rather than weakness of the heart. He is sympathetic and full of good aspirations; he is mild and kind; and he hates war. His strange delusion is the notion that the kind of world he seeks can be supported in mid-air, without a foundation. He denounces the Nazis but fails to see that they merely represent the logic of the modern position, which all of Western life has adopted to some degree. The Germans are more thorough and see the implications sooner. Modern man is, therefore, a pathetic creature—pathetic in his hope.

Many of those who have lost their Christian faith but are revolted by the experimental evidence of what happens when the concept of power culture is taken seriously are beginning to see that a civilization which prides itself on artistic and scientific development, independent of ethical considerations, may become a hell on earth. German education and German science have been promoted and organized to an almost incredible degree, and German art has been encouraged, but the truth is that these are not enough. Without something else the end is moral chaos. Since the characteristic products of the hard labor of the laboratory can be used for a variety of ends, it is no surprise that these have made possible the strategy of terror in a way utterly unknown in the world before. Without the fruit of the labors of countless honest and brilliant men the present domination of so many small countries would be absolutely impossible. This is not to say that science is to blame for what occurs, but it is to say that the belief in science as *sufficient* for the development of a good society is fatuous in the extreme.

A convincing illustration of the possible rôle of science is seen in the Nazi use of psychology. There is no subject more carefully treated in *Mein Kampf* than propaganda, especially scientifically organized propaganda. This explains the great emphasis that has been put on the work of Dr. Goebbels. Dr. Goebbels is, we have reason to know, a first-rate psychologist. He knows, to a remarkable degree, the foibles of the human heart, and he knows how to exploit them. He has made some mistakes, but his major service to a bad cause has been phenomenal. Here is as good an illustration as could be desired of scientific knowledge and insight divorced from ethical considerations. The fears of an entire nation are fostered with the kind of skill and detachment that other men employ when dealing with rats.

In a brilliant analysis of our present culture, Professor H. G. Wood has dealt directly with the claim that ethical standards can be derived from science and has used as a test case the scientific estimate of the race mysticism of the Nazis, especially the claim made for the Germans as a *Herrenvolk.* But, as Professor Wood shows, the scientific criticism of the doctrine is one thing, while the ethical criticism is another.

. . . It is a good thing that so many of our biologists and anthropologists have torn to shreds the theory of racial purity promulgated by the Nazis; but the policy of the Nazis is not wrong because the theory of blood and race assumed as its basis will not stand scientific investigation. *If the theory of blood and race advanced by the Nazis were acceptable to science, the Nazi policy would still be wrong, and we do not need the scientific refutation of their race-mysticism to see that their policy is wrong.* Their policy is wrong because if they were the Herren-volk that they claim to be, the world has the right to expect from them something very different from their present contribution to world affairs. A Herren-volk should be subject to the principle "noblesse oblige." They should justify their racial superiority by what they give to mankind, and not by what they demand; but when I say this, I am judging them by a certain standard of greatness, and this standard of greatness is not derived from any particular science or from any scientific attitude; it is derived from the Gospel. The scientific criticism of the Nazi philosophy is comparatively trivial. The criticism of it in the light of the Gospel is final.[6]

Since our age is so strongly marked by the development of science and the technical products of science, we need to engage in more searching enquiry concerning the place of science in a civilization. We soon note that, in the nature of things, science may be good but that it is always a con-

[6] H. G. Wood, *Christianity and Civilization,* p. 28.

ditional good. The goodness of science is conditional because science is an instrument and the same instrument can be used for various or contrasting ends. It is like fire, which can burn valuable libraries or warm men's dwellings with equal success. Science can help us to know the facts in most situations and it can help us to perform intended tasks, but it cannot tell us what we ought to do. Professor Wood's reasoning is so helpful at this point that it is desirable to quote him again:

If we accept as our guiding principle the second great commandment, "Thou shalt love thy neighbor as thyself," science can help us not only by providing us with means to fulfil the law, but also by defining the obligations of neighborly love in detail. But the command is not a deduction from science or the scientific attitude, and if it be denied, the scientific attitude cannot reaffirm it. Ultimate ethical principles are not deductions from natural science. Indeed the boot is on the other leg. Natural science depends for its existence and progress on the acceptance of some ethical distinctions and ethical disciplines.[7]

This last point is the one that needs most clarification now. Since science is such an undoubted good, though a conditional good, we must try to discover in which cultural situations it can flourish or is likely to flourish. It is abundantly clear that there are some kinds of life in which science either cannot flourish or will actually decline. For example, science will not be long possible in any

[7] *Ibid.,* pp. 30, 31.

society that denies complete freedom of research. Scientists will not be able to do good work over a long period if they are controlled by any consideration other than the unprejudiced search for the truth. It is particularly clear that any limitation on freedom of inquiry will lead to the decline of a university. "A university," as President Hutchins has told us, "is a place where people think. It follows that the criterion of a university is intellectual." But in a system of power culture there is another criterion that supplants the criterion of intellectual integrity.

How the limitation on freedom works in practice was made clear as early as 1936, when the University of Heidelberg held its jubilee celebration. Though the foreign representatives were relatively few, there was a strong effort to impress them, but, even so, the limitations on academic freedom were not denied. The Reich Minister of Education, Herr Bernhard Rust, sought to defend the system by saying:

National Socialism is justly described as unfriendly to science if its appraiser assumes that independence of presuppositions and freedom from bias are the essential characteristics of scientific inquiry. But this we emphatically deny. National Socialism has recognized the fact that to construct a system of knowledge without presuppositions and without certain value judgments at its foundation is totally impossible.[8]

[8] John Brown Mason, "Academic Freedom under Nazism," *Social Science*, Vol. XV, No. 4.

Value judgments are undoubtedly inescapable, but the value judgment on which science in the Western world is based is the sacredness of truth. It is incompatible with a system that breeds a disregard for objective truth or undermines the standard of personal honesty that requires a man to submit unfavorable as well as favorable evidence when he is testing a hypothesis. Science is possible because there are men engaged in it who *will not* sell out to the political boss, who *will not* falsify reports to support a preconceived notion, who *will* stay on the job even when the ordinary rewards are denied. Science, then, depends on ethical foundations, the chief of which is the unmercenary love of truth.

A consideration of the ethical foundations of science leads us to the clearest evidence that the system of power culture is bound to fail, no matter how successful it may seem for a time. It will finally fall of its own weight, because it involves inner contradictions. The power ideal in the modern world rests on the instrumental value of technics, and technical advance is impossible without faithful groundwork in the natural sciences. If truth is interpreted as referring, not to what is objectively the case, but to what advances the party or the nation, this faithful work cannot long be fostered. The best spirits will be driven out, as Einstein was driven out of Germany, and those who remain will find themselves working in an unhealthy atmosphere. Genuine science is something so delicate and so precious that it cannot thrive except under the best conditions.

The condition which, so far, has been most conducive to science is that in which the Christian world view is generally accepted.[9] Men who undertake to think God's thought after Him are working under a powerful stimulus. It is interesting to note that much of this mood carries over into the lives of men who, on the basis of the evidence with which they are acquainted, are forced to declare themselves as atheists. Frequently they have the reverent attitude toward the truth and the search for it that makes sense only in a theistic world view and is obviously inherited from such a view.[10] Why should men be so finicky about the "truth" if the only relevant considerations are our subjective desires and brute matter? Indeed, the Nazis have carried out quite rigorously the logic of the non-theistic position. In doing so they have done the rest of mankind the service of showing the dire results of adopting the non-Euclidean faith that we have already described. Their pragmatism may

[9] The supposed conflict between science and the Christian faith has been much overestimated. Even the conflict that has occurred has been no more than an episode. It is in universities that owe their origins to Christian inspiration that a great share of scientific advancement has been made.

[10] The Archbishop of Canterbury says, in his Gifford Lectures, that he attaches great importance to this point. Speaking of the sense in which Truth is august and compelling, he says: "This feeling is quite unreasonable if the order of reality is a brute fact and nothing else."—William Temple, *Nature, Man and God*, p. 250.

be a bastard pragmatism, but it at least demon-- strates to us the vast difference between a cultural system that accepts an order of objective truth and one that does not. It is a serious question whether the specific features of Western civilization that we have learned to prize are possible at all if their ancient foundations are removed. "It is perhaps a strange thing." writes Professor Flewelling, "that so little attention has as yet been paid to the necessity for moral and spiritual integrity in the scientist. In reality an integrity is called for which is no less than religious in its scope and sense of responsibility, and the field of science has never been wanting in its martyrs to the cause of truth."[11] A culture that does not encourage this kind of integrity will not have genuine science very long.

Just as some declare their faith in science without inquiring sufficiently into the structure that makes science possible, others assert that their faith is in democracy. But a democratic way of life can by no means stand alone. Its success or failure depends, not primarily on political technics, but on the un- argued principles and premises that the citizens of a democracy already espouse. Ultimately it depends on the faith of the people, and this fact is demon- strated by the failure of the most modern demo- cratic technics when the supporting faith is weak or non-existent.

[11] Ralph Tyler Flewelling, *The Survival of Western Culture*, Harper & Brothers, New York, 1943, p. 211. Professor Flewel- ling's ambitious book will reward the careful reader.

Democracy does not succeed by creating a system of counting votes. It depends far more on whether we retain the essential dignity of man. Can man, the individual, respect himself and his neighbors? If he cannot, the most elaborate system will break down. Lacking respect for himself and failing to trust others, he is easily appealed to by a demagogue who asks the citizens to trust him and him alone. Loss of the sense of human dignity leads thus directly to Caesarism. But how is this sense of human dignity to be maintained and preserved?

Just as science and political order are dependent on more fundamental considerations, so economic justice also is dependent. Professor Von Beckerath has done good service in showing how economic reconstruction is largely dependent on moral stamina. If faith in the pledged word should break down, we should have a marked lowering of the economic standard of living no matter what fine instruments of production we might invent.[12]

The question that faces mankind at this juncture is not *which civilization we like but how civilization is possible*. We are especially interested in how that civilization is possible which produces science and art and the various improvements on raw nature. The meaning of civilization, as most of us understand it, is the supremacy of reason, not merely

[12] Cf. Herbert Von Beckerath, *In Defense of the West.*

over the forces of nature, but more truly over our human dispositions.[13] This sounds like a matter of education, but the problem goes far deeper than that. Mass education brings its own dangers and may actually lead to degradation since the resultant literacy makes it easier to reach a people with propaganda. The conclusion, then, is that there can be no enduring or generally satisfying civilization apart from ethical foundations. A mere power culture will eventually cease to be a culture at all.

What would happen if worse came to worst and the moral foundations that have been so laboriously constructed in several centuries were to be destroyed, as they have already been temporarily destroyed in some parts of the West? Most of our external structure would still stand, just as most of the external structure of Rome stood after the ancient pattern was shattered. Some observers might even be impressed, for a while, with trains that run on time. But the external structure of society would be an empty shell. All combinations between different power groups would be temporary arrangements of ultimate rivals, and everyone would understand their transitory and cynical nature. There would be continual planetary civil war, either a war of bullets or a war of nerves, and most of the fine things that man has produced would eventually be destroyed. Finally, restoration might come, but

[13] Cf. Albert Schweitzer, *The Decay and Restoration of Civilization*, pp. 37 ff.

it would come only by the slow, hard way of ethical reconstruction.

Modern Western man should be wise enough to engage in this practical and necessary task while he still has allies and while he has great resources. The chief of these resources in the Western world centers in a precious cluster of ideas, which has been well described by Professor Stace as follows:

Western civilization, especially as it appears in democratic countries and institutions, has for its inner soul or substance a special and peculiar cluster of ideas. I call them a cluster because they cling together. They imply one another. The chief members of this cluster are the ideas of (1) the infinite value of the individual; (2) the equality of all men (in some sense or other); (3) individualism; (4) liberty.[14]

Modern man has many important tasks, but it is difficult to think of one more important than the maintenance, growth, and application of this cluster. The question how this can be done will be approached in the next chapter.

[14] W. T. Stace, *The Destiny of Western Man*, p. 124.

CHAPTER III

The Impotence of Ethics

Here is no water but only rock.
Rock and no water and the sandy road.

T. S. Eliot

《《《《 》》》》

WE HAVE inherited, in the Western world, a cluster of ideas which we regard as precious and about which there is more agreement than superficially appears. Apart from a conscious rejection of these ideas, such as is described in the previous chapter, it is generally agreed throughout the West that human individuality is precious and that things must be used for the sake of man rather than man for the sake of things. When it comes to actual practice, we may depart from this standard rather markedly, but there is little argument about the principle. Furthermore, we hold that the state, being only a human device for the benefit of man, is not an object of absolute loyalty and ought not to be. The state exists for man, not man for the state. Most of us give hearty consent to Edmund Burke's dictum that "all political power which is set over men ought to be in some way or other exercised ultimately for their benefit." Acceptance of these ideas constitutes, in general, what we call humanism; and, whatever else we are, most of us are humanists in this broad sense.

Another part of the cluster of ideas, to which general assent is given, concerns human equality. We hold that there is no favored race and no nation which ought to be dominant. Consequently, racial discrimination and all forms of slavery are believed to be wrong. We assert this proposition with a bit more hesitation than might be expected of those who mean what they say, but in any case *we are ashamed to deny it*.

A third part of this precious cluster is the concept of peace as the desirable condition for mankind. Very little of the Western world is pacifist in the extreme sense of refusal to participate in war after war is declared, but large portions of the Western world are pacifist in the sense that they hate war and all its works, and they participate in it only with troubled consciences and heaviness of heart. It is generally agreed amongst us that war is a sorry necessity at best, always a means to an end, and that the end is peace. We do not glory in war or maintain that it is needed as a stimulus to the heroic in man. We fight when we must to clear away the barriers to peace, and we make peace as rapidly and as securely as our conditions permit. War, in the Western mind, is an unfortunate interlude and nothing more.

On all this, we say, there is substantial agreement. This agreement has come not merely from the judgment of the rank and file, but even more strikingly from our moral philosophers who have given their lives to critical inquiry. Though our moral philosophers have differed in many details, especially in regard to the sources of moral judgment, they have agreed amazingly in regard to what men ought to do. Thus there is very little disagreement with Kant's famous dictum: "So act as to treat humanity, whether in thine own person or in that of any other, in every case as an end withal, never as a means only." Since this cannot be a genuine basis of conduct unless it depends, in turn, on a true experience of personal fellowship, the one permanently valid form of the categorical imperative, so Western man believes, is "Thou shalt love thy neighbor as thyself." Most thoughtful members of our Western society will give hearty assent when the highest official of the Church of England says that "the essence of morality is personal fellowship or respect for persons as persons."[1]

Precious as this heritage is, there is grave question whether it can be made either to continue or to prevail. How can anything so mild be maintained in open competition with *Blut und Boden*? The problem is vastly accentuated by the fact that great numbers who accept this Western creed accept it halfheartedly and conventionally, while those who

[1] William Temple, *Nature, Man and God*, p. 254.

espouse a creed of blood or soil or race or nation or class usually espouse it with fanatical zeal. We take our creed for granted; we have little interest in how it came to be; and we assume uncritically that it will naturally survive. This is the pathetic faith of Western man in the middle of the twentieth century, a faith utterly unjustified by experience.

We can take no comfort from the fact that the pseudo paganism, which we have described under the category of power culture, is perverse and fundamentally decadent. The barbarism is, indeed, synthetic, as Reinhold Niebuhr has told us, but *it is not weak.* "For the first time in history," writes Niebuhr, "the barbarisms which threaten civilization have been generated in the heart of a decadent civilization. The barbarism which threatens us is 'synthetic' rather than genuine."[2] But, synthetic as it is, it is far too strong an adversary for the easy-going Westerner who says, complacently, that he has worked out a "philosophy" which is personally satisfactory to him and that he believes in being kind.

As we have already pointed out, the system of power culture must eventually fall because of its inner contradictions, and in this we *can* take comfort, but our sense of comfort is premature if we suppose the failure of one evil system means the reinstitution of that which sensitive men have most

[2] Reinhold Niebuhr, *Christianity and Power Politics*, New York, 1940, p. 118.

prized. *Evil structures are indeed precarious, but evil structures are not automatically followed by something better.*

One of the most disturbing of the parables of Jesus is the parable of the empty house.[3] The house, we are told, was emptied of the unclean spirit that had occupied it and was swept and garnished. *But it could not remain empty.* Not only did the original evil spirit return, but seven other devils, worse than the first, accompanied him. We have already seen this development in parts of our culture, and we shall see it in other parts unless we follow a more intelligent course of action. The empty condition, spiritually, is a condition of the greatest danger.

The danger of emptiness is seen vividly in the desire for unity and community. With the breakdown of legitimate bases of solidarity, men, and especially young men, could not remain satisfied with the amorphous heterogeneity of atomistic individualism. They longed to belong to something, and thus arose the new solidarities, which are of so perverted a kind as to menace the future of the human race.

Here, then, is our predicament: We have inherited precious ethical convictions that seem to us to be profound, central, and essential. But they have a curious inefficacy. *They are noble, but they are impotent.* We are amazed, by contrast, at the

[3] Matthew, 12:43-45.

power that an alternative creed can engender. It is clear that something more is needed, that moral convictions, while necessary to the good life, are not sufficient. Perhaps an analysis of recent experience will give us our clue as to what this "something more" is.

Most careful observers agree that the two systems of life which have recently inspired the youth of Germany and of Russia are quasi-religious. They are much more than economics, and they are much more than politics. They are undoubtedly inadequate as religions, and in large measure *false* religions, but they have the effect that only religion can have. Millions now dying on both sides of the eastern front are dying for a *faith*. When we say that the system of which Adolf Hitler has been the prophet (and that, to an increasing degree, is his rôle) is fundamentally religious, we mean that it includes the element of absolute commitment which is everywhere the distinguishing mark of religion. The sad truth is that this commitment can be given to base objects more easily than it can be given to the Living God.

We understand much of the distinction between religion and other phases of our lives when we sense the profound difference between faith and belief. Faith is closer to courage than it is to intellectual assent. Faith is easily understood by the gambler, as both Blaise Pascal and Donald Hankey knew, because the gambler stands to win or lose by his play. This was brought out in Kirsopp Lake's now classic definition, "Faith is not belief in spite of evidence, but life in scorn of consequences." *Faith*, as the plain man knows, *is not belief without proof, but trust without reservations*.

The lesson of history is that those lacking such a faith are no match for those inspired by such a faith, *whatever its object*. The fearful aspect of the present situation is that those who have inherited the major tradition of the West now *have an ethic without a religion, whereas they are challenged by millions who have a religion without an ethic*. The former group will win the war, because they have the preponderance of men and resources, as well as a fortunate alliance with Russia, but that is by no means the end of the story. We should be gullible indeed if we supposed that mere military victory would end the powerful threat of the faith which is proposed as a successor to the religion of the West.

Little do we know what evil faith may grip our people when the war is over. Since men cannot live long without a faith, the choice is always a choice between competing faiths. The only practical alternative to an evil faith is a better faith. Though this is the lesson of history, we are now trying the utterly precarious experiment, in which the odds are against us, of attempting to maintain our culture by loyalty to the Christian ethic without a corresponding faith in the Christian religion that produced it.

The characteristic intellectual, at least in English-speaking countries, is much influenced by the Christian ethic. He is brave and kind, he tries to obey the Ten Commandments, or in any case the last six, and he gives full intellectual assent to the Golden Rule. If he thinks seriously about the Hebrew Decalogue, he thinks that the ancients put the commandments in the wrong order. He would put the moral commandments first and the strictly religious ones last.[4] He would seldom be aware that, in this regrouping, his judgment is in sharp opposition to the judgment of Jesus on the same subject.

The average Western intellectual appears to think of himself not merely as a humanist, which we all are, but as a humanist and no more. As such he is not necessarily antagonistic to religion, since there is obviously no contradiction between interest in human values and faith in God. Indeed, the main historic tradition in humanism has been Christian humanism, consciously refreshed at Christian sources. But, though the modern humanist does not oppose religion, he usually does something worse—*he ignores it*. He acts in practice as though God does not exist and, without arguing the matter, assumes rather uncritically that religion is some-

[4] A large class in an American university was asked, recently, to regroup the commandments in order of importance. More than 90 per cent of the students put the first two commandments last.

thing outgrown. The result is that much of our current humanism is atheistic in practice, though not in theory. It is supposed that the fruits of the ancient faith can be enjoyed without attention to its roots.

Since the fashionable humanism of our day does not lack for able and eloquent spokesmen, we can select representatives with ease. They were numerous in pre-Hitler Germany, and they are numerous in the democracies now, though they are not so numerous as they were before the storm broke. If we were writing in England, it would be suitable to use as representative the writings of Julian Huxley or C. E. M. Joad. In America, an equally suitable representative is Alexander Meiklejohn, whose brilliant career as a philosopher and public servant entitles his words to respect. Meiklejohn has recently published a book called *Education between Two Worlds*, in which he espouses the creed of ethics minus religion with great clarity and discrimination. The reviews have shown that his following is great, especially in educational circles.

Though Meiklejohn is representative of the current tendency in one way, there is another way in which he is not representative. He is representative in the content of his belief or unbelief, but he is unrepresentative in his expression of it. He is an excellent spokesman who says clearly what so many think, but think in a confused or truncated manner. In particular, he sees, better than does the average man, the dangers of the position he champions. Most of the atheism of our time is unconscious, unargued, and unexplicit, whereas Meiklejohn's atheism, while it is unargued, is at least conscious and explicit:

> The cosmos as a whole, out of which human life emerges, gives no evidence of being, or wishing to be, intelligent. The human spirit is alone in an otherwise non-human, nonspiritual universe. Whatever it has, or may ever have, of sensitiveness, of wisdom, of generosity, of freedom, of justice, it has made, it will make, for itself.[5]

The confidence with which such a sweeping statement is made surprises us, especially in view of the brilliant contemporary studies that *do* show evidence of Mind outside our little planet,[6] but perhaps it has not occurred to writers of this type that there might be exciting new thinking in contemporary theology. It is to Meiklejohn's credit that he has some idea of the gravity of the human problem which such a change in conviction entails. "If we can no longer believe in God," he asks, "can we maintain, can we carry on, the civilization which was founded on that belief?"

Perhaps no question of this kind is ever permanently answered, but it is important to point out that there is a great body of evidence which suggests a negative answer to Meiklejohn's question.

[5] Alexander Meiklejohn, *Education between Two Worlds*, Harper & Brothers, New York, 1942, p. 200.
[6] See Temple, *op. cit.*, Chapter V.

And the chief evidence is to be found in the actual experience of men, especially in our part of the twentieth century. Since there is so much evidence of the moral decay that follows a loss of theistic conviction and so little evidence of the maintenance of civilization apart from this conviction, the burden of proof is on the person who answers Meiklejohn's question in the affirmative. For the most part he has nothing more than speculation to offer as against the actual logic of events.

It must be remembered that there were many people in Germany who, during the time that Hitlerism was rising, accepted the benevolent and humane creed which Meiklejohn champions. But their humane creed was impotent in conflict with the narrow doctrine of race. The country seemingly was divided between those who embraced a humane creed with no enthusiasm and those who embraced the dogma of synthetic barbarism with abounding enthusiasm. *Wherever this situation occurs, the crude doctrine will win.* The excellence of humane sentiments is no guarantee of success, at least in the short run. If men are told the Golden Rule, they listen and give assent and *do nothing*. If they are told they belong to a master race, they proceed to demonstate the truth of the statement.

The notion that an atheist is an evil man has little justification in experience. A pragmatist like John Dewey is often good and kind. The chief criticism to be leveled at the atheistic moralist is not that he is wicked, but that he is naïve. His assumption that the kind of life he prizes can stand up rootless against the contemporary storm has nothing to commend it in the actual experience of men. The impotence of contemporary moralism arises from the fact that "we are trying to maintain a political valuation of man which had roots in a religious understanding of him, when that religious understanding has been forgotten."[7]

The cluster of ideas that we prize in our Western culture has been with us so long that we often forget how these ideas first came into the world. We owe a great deal, of course, to the classic cultures of Greece and Rome, but we tend to read back into the ancient literature conceptions that the classic authors did not really hold. Not until the rise of Christianity did the ancient world discountenance infanticide; likewise, it was Christianity "that ended the scandal of taking human life for sport,"[8] and altered the status of women. Humanitarian ideals existed in classic culture, but the humanitarianism we prize in the West owes most of its original impetus to the gospel. It is interesting to note that this is the conclusion to which Alfred Loisy came, on the basis of his immense scholarship.

The best thing in present-day societies is the feeling for humanity which has come to us from the gospel

[7] William Paton, *The Church and the New Order*, Student Christian Movement Press, London, 1941, p. 152.

[8] H. G. Wood, *Christianity and Civilization*, p. 11. Professor Wood's other examples are instructive.

and which we owe to Christianity. You will object that we have made this Christianity ourselves or at least perfected it. That is true, but it is not under the predominant influence of Greece and Rome that we have perfected it; it is by lending an ear to the voice of Jerusalem to which the ancient world finally listened, finding that it could not continue morally, humanely, by its own wisdom.[9]

Even Meiklejohn, who makes no claim to being a Christian, appreciates perfectly what the source of so many of our humane ideals is, and he is especially clear about this in regard to the principles of education. In his account of the influence of Comenius, he points out that the advanced educational notions of Comenius came directly as applications of his Christian faith. His faith in God, as revealed by Christ, made him support a double universalism, the unity of knowledge and the unity of mankind. The strength of the educational idealism of Comenius came from the fact that it had roots. "Comenius believes in God," writes Meiklejohn. "Therefore he is a democrat. Therefore the unified study of the world is for him a normal part of the healthy living of every human being."[10]

The terrible danger of our time consists in the fact that ours is a *cut-flower civilization*. Beautiful as cut flowers may be, and much as we may use our ingenuity to keep them looking fresh for a while, they will eventually die, and they die because

---

[9] Alfred Loisy, *La Morale humaine*, p. 251.
[10] Meiklejohn, *op. cit.*, p. 27.

they are severed from their sustaining roots. We are trying to maintain the dignity of the individual apart from the deep faith that every man is made in God's image and is therefore precious in God's eyes. Certainly we cannot maintain this if we accept a metaphysical doctrine that refuses to admit any difference in kind between a living mind and a mechanical structure. We do not reverence a mechanical structure—we *use* it. We are trying to keep the notion of freedom, especially freedom of speech, while we give up the basic convictions on which freedom depends. Freedom of research, for example, loses all its point unless there is an objective truth to which the scientist is loyal. Freedom of moral action likewise loses its point unless there is an objective right that the individual seeks to follow, whatever the personal cost. But belief in objective truth and belief in objective right are part of what we mean by belief in God.

If there is any suspicion that our standards are of our own making, weakness is bound to set in. *Those who make can also set aside*. What we need in order to give power is not an assertion of our own ideals, but contact with the eternally real. The ideal may be our own imaginary construction, wholly devoid of cosmic support. What men need, if they are to overcome their lethargy and weakness, is some contact with the real world in which moral values are centered in the nature of things. This is the love of God, for which men have long shown themselves willing to live or to die. The only sure way in which we can transcend our human relativities is by obedience to the absolute and eternal God.

Our major tradition is one in which men have had the courage to be free and to uphold the sacredness of individual personality because of their religious convictions. The appeal of democracy is not very great if we are concerned *merely* with democracy. It is easy, then, to make democracy seem ridiculous, as the apologists of totalitarianism have already done so effectively. But democracy has great attractive power if its appeal is *derivative*, if it is the practical application of profound convictions about God and man as it was for so many of the founding fathers of both British and American democracy in the seventeenth century.

The trouble with so many of our fine ideals is that they tend to be *abstract*. What, actually, do we mean when we speak of the love of humanity? We certainly do not mean that we love all the existent miserable people in the world, most of whom we have never seen. The abstract duty of being humane is not such as to dominate men's lives, but there is something else which *can* dominate them. We get a hint concerning what this is when we note that Jesus apparently said nothing about "the indefeasible value of the individual," but He did say that not a sparrow "shall fall without your

Father,"[11] and "take heed that ye despise not one
of these little ones. . . ."[12] Here is concreteness that
gives power.

An ordinary man, merely in and of himself, is
not of so great worth and may be a very poor
creature. We shall not make an effective answer to
the apostles of blood and soil by pointing to *him*.
But there is something else to which we *can* point,
as the late William Paton said in a memorable para-
graph:

But if this humble and obscure man is in reality one
whom God has made, whom He has made in love, so
that he shall never know peace except in loving God
in return; if this man is one to whom God speaks; if
this man is the object of a Divine solicitude so great
that the Word became flesh for his salvation, the Son
of God died for him—if this be true, then this humble
and obscure man has a link with eternity, with the
creative love that made the world. He cannot then be
rightly treated as a cog in a machine, or a sample of a
racial blood-stream, or one of the individual atoms that
make up a nation.[13]

It is especially in our Christian tradition that we
find the power which is so conspicuously lacking
in mere moralism. We must not forget that, in the
Roman Empire, Christ won, and won against tre-
mendous odds. He won because the faith in Christ
really changed the lives of countless weak men and
made them bold as lions. He has taken poor crea-

[11] Matthew, 10:29.
[12] Matthew, 18:10.
[13] Paton, *op. cit.*, pp. 150, 151.

tures who could not even understand the language of moral philosophy and shaken the world through them.

This has been said brilliantly by John Baillie:

> Christ did not come to earth to tell us merely what we ought to do; He came to do something for us. He came not merely to exhort but to help. He did not come to give us good advice. That, if it were no more than that, was possibly not a thing of which we stood greatly in need, for there are always plenty of people who are ready with their advice. Advice is cheap, but what Christ offered us was infinitely costly. It was the power of God unto salvation.[14]

It is easy enough to hate Hitler, but what is it that we propose as an alternative to his proposal for mankind? We now have a good opportunity to know, since we see suggestions daily in our propaganda sheets and even more in the expensive advertisements that so many large commercial firms are using for the building of morale, now that they have nothing to sell to the average reader. They all say about the same thing. We are to oppose the new paganism in the name of humanity, liberty, brotherhood, the sacredness of the individual soul. These are all very fine, but the question is whether they go far enough. John Baillie's analysis is so good that his words should be cited again:

> These indeed are the ideals of the Christian ages, or some of them, or at least they sound very like them, but in the Christian Ages they were all deeply rooted in something bigger and grander, in something that

[14] John Baillie, *Invitation to Pilgrimage*, p. 51.

was no mere ideal but an eternal reality. They were rooted in the love of God as manifest in Jesus Christ our Lord. . . . It was Christ who taught us the indefeasible value of the individual soul. It was Christ who taught us of *fraternité* when He said, 'One is your Master, even Christ, and all ye are brethren'; and St. Paul when he said that 'we, being many, are one body in Christ, and every one member one of another.' Hence the doubt that keeps raising itself in my mind when I read these fine pronouncements about our ideals . . . is whether these ideals have sufficient strength of conviction in them, or sufficient power of survival, in face of so powerful a contrary force, when they are no longer allowed to breathe their native air or draw daily sustenance from their original source.[15]

Moralizing cannot stand against a burning faith, even when that faith is an evil and perverted one. It is almost as ineffective as an umbrella in a tornado. The only way in which we can overcome our impotence and save our civilization is by the discovery of a sufficient faith. Goodness we must have, but the way to goodness is to find our peace in the love of God who, as the Source of goodness, makes us know that, even at best, we are not really good. This is the peace that passes understanding, though it is not a peace that negates the understanding.

Some of the hardest problems of our day are moral problems, rather than economic or political ones; but, moral problems as they are, many of them cannot be solved except on a religious basis. One example of this is provided by the problem of

[15] *Ibid.*, pp. 125, 126.

racial antipathy, a problem that has been accentuated rather than diminished in the recent development of our civilization. So great is the hold of race prejudice on men's minds that it must be counteracted by something powerful and revolutionary. Men do not transcend the prejudice and hatred based on race by physical proximity or even by the reasonable evidence that all need each other. What is needed is a genuine conversion, striking at the roots of the sinful pride on which race hatred thrives. The great known examples of history in which this kind of animosity has been really overcome have been chiefly religious examples, like that of John Woolman. In all honesty we are compelled to state that religion does not have this effect universally, but that we should hardly expect, knowing what we do about the ability of the human heart to keep its cherished hatreds. What we can honestly state is that the religious approach is more likely to be successful in our particular culture than is any other. The reason for the greater probability of the success of the religious approach is that the problem is fundamentally a religious problem. Race hatred comes, primarily, not from ignorance, but from *sin*. We will not accept all men as brothers until we are really humble, and we are not really humble until we measure ourselves by the revelation of the Living God.

A second relevant example of a problem which is essentially insoluble except on the religious level is that provided by our sense of national destiny. In many ways the democratic nations will be in greater danger after the war than those nations which have been more obviously guilty. What if *we* should begin to feel like a *Herrenvolk*, sure of our superior virtue as well as of our superior power? Since we shall not have the sobering experience of defeat, what is there to keep us steady? One of our major debts to the thinking of Reinhold Niebuhr is at precisely this point. "There is no cure," writes Niebuhr, "for the pride of a virtuous nation but pure religion. The pride of a powerful nation may be humbled by the impotence which defeat brings. The pride of a virtuous nation cannot be humbled by moral and political criticisms because in comparative terms it may actually be virtuous."[16]

The only experience we know that is revolutionary enough both to support the downcast nation and to chasten the victorious nation is the sense of existing under the eternal Providence of the Living God. In this, as Lincoln discovered in the tragic days of the Civil War, we find a level of experience which does the seemingly impossible of making us firm in the right, "as God gives us to see the right," but also humble because we are conscious that "the Almighty has his own purposes." It is religion and religion alone that does this for men. For this reason we can never have a real civilization without it.

[16] Reinhold Niebuhr, "Anglo-Saxon Destiny and Responsibility," *Christianity and Crisis*, October 4, 1943, Vol. III, No. 16, p. 3.

CHAPTER IV

The Insufficiency of Individual Religion

~~~~~~

I am forced to confess that what I once despised I now praise
unreservedly.

ALBERT EINSTEIN

《《《《　》》》》

THE chief argument of this book up to this
point represents the thinking of great numbers
in the Western world and will presumably, therefore, be convincing to many readers who have
given serious thought to the problem of the reconstruction of civilization in our time. The characteristic modern is not a sheer pagan and certainly will
not be attracted to the claims of synthetic barbarism as presented by either its major or its minor
prophets. Too many centuries of Christian culture
have intervened between pagan times and our own
for the resuscitation of paganism to succeed where
it has been consciously attempted.

Just as most of the citizens of the Western world
reject paganism, when they give the matter any
attention, so likewise do they recognize the unten-
ability of power culture. The experience of the

last decade has been sufficient to convince great numbers, if they were not convinced before, that civilized life cannot prosper, or even survive, without the undergirding of strong ethical convictions. The neglect of ethics means decay, no matter how great the initial power may be.

The average modern, we believe, goes at least one step further than this. As he is not a pagan, so he is not irreligious. He will agree that mere ethics is unable to produce the required regeneration, and, humanist as he is, he sees that the strength of humanism comes from something beyond humanism. The need of religion, if our culture is to be saved, is widely recognized, not merely by theologians, but by men concerned with science, with the humanities, and with the social sciences.[1] Theoretical and explicit atheism is comparatively rare and is frequently denied by those who might be supposed to espouse it. The belief in God may be both weak and attenuated, but there is great reluctance to renounce it wholly.

Not only is the average modern not irreligious; he is also not anti-Christian. He recognizes, when he thinks about it, that he stands within the Christian tradition, and he has no practical acquaintance with any other. He may never read the Bible, but the value judgments of the Bible, and especially the gospel, have become in large measure his own

[1] See Robert S. Lynd, *Knowledge for What*, Princeton, 1939, especially pp. 239 ff.

standards, even though he gives them little conscious attention. Twentieth century man, if pressed for an answer, admits that he believes in a moral order, that he believes in religion, and that he believes in the Christian religion, but there he stops. He is trying to live in the midst of the world storm, not as an adherent of paganism and not as an opponent of the Christian faith, but as one who adheres to that faith in the most vague and tenuous manner conceivable. *He claims to be a shareholder in the Christian corporation, but the stock has been watered almost to the vanishing point and is held, moreover, by absentee owners.*

If we are to speak truly to our age, therefore, we can assume, not (1) the complete ignorance of Christian principles, such as existed in the decaying civilization of early Greece and Rome; (2) the thoroughgoing knowledge and acceptance of Christian principles, such as existed in the time of most of our grandparents; or (3) the vigorous antagonism to the gospel, such as now exists among those who accept either the Marxist or the Fascist interpretation of history; but (4) a vague and tenuous residuum of Christian piety, devoid of any intention of doing anything about it. To know our spiritual situation is something, for it at least saves us from dealing with straw men. The hopeful side of the picture is that the number of persons who are disturbed by this state of affairs, because they doubt if a vague and tenuous piety can sustain a civilization, is obviously growing.

The notion that we cannot have a decent world apart from a faith sufficient to inspire high ethical standards and action is now gaining ground. Not long ago the majority of our educated citizens appeared to suppose that ethical standards are self-supporting and that a humanistic culture is self-sustaining. Now most of them know better, having been convinced not so much by the logic of words as by the logic of events. They have been led by experience to conclude that the only power in human life able to counterbalance the dark and divisive faiths of our time is a still stronger faith, a faith concerned with Reality rather than human wishes.

The question before anyone who cares about the fate of men and women in the modern world is the question how a really saving faith can be encouraged and promoted. How can modern man, whose world seems to topple about him, regain a living faith in the Living God, so that he can feel once more both the dignity of his own life and the dignity of the lives of his fellow men—everywhere?

In this great task the work of those who use their mental powers to show that the theistic hypothesis is true is, of course, absolutely essential. No matter how helpful a faith is, if it is not true, we want nothing of it. We would rather go to pieces

on the basis of honesty than to patch up a civilization on the basis of fiction or wishful thinking. But
that, fortunately, is not the point now most press-
ing. The rational arguments for theism were never
stronger than they are today and never better
presented. There are no philosophical or scientific
discoveries that have outmoded them. The point
to make now is that intellectual convincement,
necessary as it is and valuable as it is, is not sufficient.
For faith to become concrete it must be embodied
in a human society. Separated, individual believers
will not be able to make any headway against the
present storm.

What is sobering in this regard is the fact that
so many of the intellectual leaders of our time are
willing to stop with intellectual convincement. Distinguished men of letters, essayists, novelists, and
poets, have recently asserted their conviction that
the only thing which can save our sagging culture
is a revival of religious faith, but many of these men
make no contact whatever with the particular organizations in their own communities which are
dedicated to the nourishment of the very faith they
declare necessary for our salvation. There are
countless people who would resent being considered
irreligious but who reject the practice of group
religion. "I have my own religion," has become a
cliché. Some prefer to say they believe in Christianity but not in Churchianity. In short, they believe
in religion, but not in the church. They are keenly

aware of the weaknesses of the church as they have
known it and they propose the experiment of
churchless religion. Since this way of thinking is
so widespread, we must consider it seriously.

When we think of the awful need of humanity
at this hour, it seems almost grotesque to turn to
the church for help, if by the church we mean not
some idealization, but the actual human organizations we know. On the face of it, the hypothesis
that the church can play a major part in saving
civilization seems an outrageous hypothesis. While
it is manifestly true that there is a great faith which
has long been the secret of life in Western man,
does not the ordinary church, whether in New
York, Middletown, or Gopher Prairie, provide such
a caricature of this faith that it is really a joke?
What mankind desperately needs is Justice, Mercy,
and Truth, but what we are offered is some ugly
stained-glass windows and a holy tone and a collec-
tion plate full of dimes.

Any candid observer will agree that most of the
popular criticisms of the church are justified. It
has hypocrites in it, and it is weak when it ought
to be strong. But the urgent question is the question of a better alternative when the nature of our
present crisis is such that our option is a forced
option. The only live alternatives to the church are
the pseudo religions of totalitarianism or *vague
religiosity*. Since we have already seen reason to
reject one of these, the other, i.e., vague religiosity,

is really the only alternative to the church that our present culture offers. Loyal identification with the church may have difficulties, but the alternative position may have more. Since no position on any fundamental question is wholly free from difficulties, the path of wisdom lies not in rejecting a position because it is found to have difficulties but rather in making an honest comparison of difficulties involved in alternatives. John Baillie's report on the effectiveness of this approach is interesting and instructive:

> I am happy to count among my own friends a rather remarkable number of men of high intellectual distinction who have returned to the full Christian outlook after years of defection from it, and I should say that in practically every case the renewed hospitality of their minds to Christian truth came about through their awakening to the essential untenability of the alternative positions which they had been previously attempting to occupy.[2]

What, then, are the real difficulties of the position in which so many of our sensitive contemporaries have halted, the position of the man who has his own religion but who does not throw his efforts into the establishment and enlargement of any religious group or church? The first important difficulty is the moral one that such a person is a parasite. He is taking more than he is giving. He lives in a world many of the desirable features of which have come about by the slow, painful efforts

[2] John Baillie, *Invitation to Pilgrimage*, p. 15.

of just such groups of weak and sinful men as he now refuses to join. Since the position of the social parasite is one that cannot be universalized, it is indefensible to the sensitive conscience when the true position is made clear. Consequently, it is desirable to put as forcibly as we can the following query: *Do I profit by a spiritual movement and yet dissociate myself deliberately from the practical task of keeping it going when my help is needed?*

A second difficulty, closely allied with that of parasitism, concerns family life. The moral foundations of our culture, which organized religion has done so much to maintain, are often reasonably secure for one generation, even when actual sharing in the corporation is given up. Sometimes, under favorable conditions, it is secure longer, but those who engage in personal counseling are aware of the constant problem of the religiously detached family in which the parents are amazed at the moral bankruptcy of their children. They cannot see why their children fail to have the same standards as their own, but in truth they have denied their children any practical contact with the ongoing tradition that is chiefly concerned with keeping these alive in our culture. A strong religious movement often has enough momentum to carry over in effect for one generation, but seldom for two. The highly publicized Hollywood type of morality may not actually characterize Hollywood as a whole, but it is what we have a right to expect and what we actually find in many families that have drifted away from organized religious influence.

Those who are concerned today with the nurture of student religious life report consistently that the best work in holding the loyalty of students is carried on by those denominations which constitute a self-conscious minority, so that the members feel that they have much in common with one another. Critics of such faiths as Christian Science and Mormonism cannot but be impressed with the beneficent effect that the reality of group life has on many young people. They present a sharp contrast to the rank and file of students, most of whom call themselves Protestants merely because they are neither Roman Catholic nor Jewish and who often have little appreciation of a heritage that is precious.

There are millions of families in which the parents believe in God and live virtuous lives but in which, inasmuch as they are separated from organized religion, the children miss the steadying influence of those institutional practices which serve as constant reminders of what otherwise it is easy to forget. Young lives are formed, not chiefly by the intellectual beliefs of their parents, of which they may be wholly ignorant, but far more by family practices, such as attendance at public worship, which become habitual and are eventually unconscious influences of incalculable importance.

It is historically correct to say that Christianity

has never been a saving force in civilization when it has been looked upon as a set of noble precepts which men may observe in isolation. In the beginning the Christian faith was, above all, a fellowship. In the decaying empire of Rome there arose a fellowship so powerful that, for a while, Christians had all things in common. The fellowship was not always perfect, as the Corinthian Letters of St. Paul so clearly demonstrate, but that it should *be* a fellowship was central to the gospel.

The basic difficulty with vague religiosity is that human beings are weak and fallible and need artificial or consciously constructed supports. It is theoretically possible to be a good man without participation in the life of a religious community, but in practice the difficulties are enormous. We know what we ought to do, but we need reminders; we believe in a moral order, but we need inspiration and fellowship. We are small indeed, and we need to participate in something bigger than we are. The person who says so proudly that he has his own religion and consequently has no need of the church is committing what has been well called "the angelic fallacy." If we *were* angels, we might not need artificial help, but, being men, we normally do need it. And, whether we need it or not, others need it and we have some responsibility to them.

By participation in an ongoing religious community, particularly of the type we know in the

Western world, an isolated individual is partly lifted above himself, not only because he may, in a group, be more recipient of God's help, but also because he there shares in the distilled wisdom of our race. Week after week he hears the reading of great classics, such as the Psalms or the parables of Jesus, so that the total impact is great indeed. The reading can hardly be so poor as to spoil utterly the noble words. He shares in ancient hymns that weak men like himself have used for generations. He may still find that his highest experiences come to him as he walks alone with his dog, but these experiences are more likely to come to him if he walks with the richness of memory that participation in the ongoing community makes possible.

Finally, our vague religiosity faces an insuperable difficulty in that it provides no way by which the precious insights of our religious heritage are to be maintained. Had we always been limited to individual religion, like that which is fashionable now, we should not even be aware of the great testimonies which have survived so many crises and which the average individualist cherishes. Apart from the church, we should not have kept the Bible or the great hymns or the great prayers or even the very notion of the gospel.

Poor and weak as it is, the church may become the means of our cultural salvation because, with all its human mistakes, it includes certain contributions that otherwise the world may lose and that men have actually lost temporarily in some areas. The great testimonies, which it is the mission of the church to make and without which human life would be even more savage and degraded than it now is, are many, but four are of paramount importance in the reconstruction of civilization.

(1) *The first great testimony that the church makes in all times is that of equality before God.* Because every man, whatever his color, his knowledge, his station, or his financial standing, is a child of God, there is a profound level at which men are equal. They are not equal in that they have the same powers, but they are equal in that each is equally accountable. The upshot of this doctrine, perhaps the most disturbing that the human mind can hold, is that king and commoner are equally subject to the moral law. The result of this is bound to be democracy or something very much like it.

According to the gospel, the king is as much subject to the moral law as is the humblest subject, *because he did not make it.* It is grounded in the nature of things, which is to say it is part of the will of God. So long as there is a suggestion that some nations or some persons are above the law, there can never be a decent world, for then there is no brake on sheer power. The conviction that no nation and no person is above the law is the contribution of the Judaeo-Christian revelation to the whole world. The ancient Hebrews saw it in a way that would be shocking to us if we were not already so familiar with the idea. The Hebrews were a people among whom even King David could be judged for his cowardly treatment of the husband of Bathsheba. This testimony has come over into the Christian tradition and has been at the base of countless revolutions. Slavery and social stratification and entrenched privilege are of long standing in human society but they are never really secure so long as the gospel is known.

(2) *The second great testimony is the testimony for peace.* We take this for granted as wholly natural until we are stabbed awake by contemporary prophets who reject the gospel and hold that a condition of war is better, lifting and cleansing a nation. Actually the Christian teaching about peace is at variance with many other cultural traditions and could easily have been lost, apart from conscious fostering. The major Christian tradition has not been pacifism, in the sense of refusal to share in any war, but it has been a testimony for peace in the sense that war is seen as a necessary evil at best and never something in which to glory. It has frequently been accepted as the least of alternative evils but seldom as a positive good.[3]

[3] Excellent historical treatments of this subject are available, especially Umphrey Lee, *The Historic Church and Modern Pacifism*, Abingdon-Cokesbury Press, New York, 1943, and C. J. Cadoux, *The Early Church and the World*, T. & T. Clark, Edinburgh, 1925.

Here the position of Augustine is representative. It was his conviction that the Christian must always contemplate wars with *mental pain* and that "if any one either endures or thinks of them without mental pain, his is a more miserable plight still, for he thinks himself happy because he has lost all human feeling."[4]

It is the sad truth that wars have raged intermittently in Christendom and that the present conflict, the worst yet, has broken out in Europe, which has been under Christian influence for at least a millennium and a half; but the Christian faith has never accepted this situation or failed to deplore it. Given the inventions of our day, life might be even worse if there were not the leavening influence for peace, which shows itself in the renewed determination, on the part of millions, to try to make a world in which war is no longer a recurrent phenomenon. But the point to remember is that these millions are voicing a conviction which it has been the rôle of the church to foster for centuries. The world is bad enough *with* the leaven; it is frightening to contemplate what it might become *without* the leaven.

(3) *The third great testimony of the church is that of universality.* Though the church itself is a fractured body, it has never lost sight of the fact that it *is* a body, namely, the body of Christ. The notion of the Church Universal has been main-

[4] *The City of God*, XIX, vii.

tained. Actually the degree to which the natural divisiveness of mankind has been transcended has been very great. Men of all colors and all nationalities worship together and maintain bonds of friendship across boundaries, even in wartime. Men of every nationality, in all churches, listen to the same gospel, sing the same hymns, read the same Bible, and revere the same Lord.

The situation in regard to the testimony for universality is similar to that in regard to the testimony for peace, in that both have seemingly been honored chiefly in the breach and yet both have been maintained as leaven.

Man is naturally divisive and would be more so than he is were there not a conscious fostering of the universal principle of essential oneness. Our faith has *never* fully succeeded in bringing together men of various nations and races as one family conscious of their common origin and destiny, but it has never ceased to preach that this is the true way. There has been in the world for many centuries a continuous society devoted, not to the glorification of one race or nation or class, but to the notion that Jew and Gentile, Greek and Barbarian, Oriental and Occidental are really brothers because they are all children of a common Father. We have denied this in practice by slavery, by racial discrimination, and in a thousand other ways, but the leaven has been always at work, so that we cannot contemplate these things with equanimity or complacency. The contribution of the church to civilization is not to be measured so much by the actual degree of unity it has achieved in mankind as by the manner in which it has kept alive the ideal of world unity. Racial discrimination can never be wholly acceptable to a people who have heard from their youth that God has "made of one blood all nations of men for to dwell on all the face of the earth. . . ."[5] There is no evidence or even likelihood that this testimony would have been preserved apart from the action of the organized body of believers. Separated individuals could not have done it.

(4) *The fourth great testimony is that of renunciation of worldly pride.* This, also, appears to have been honored in the breach, in that we find the emergence of power politics in Christian countries and even in the church, which has sometimes aped the world by the honor it gives to its "dignitaries." But here, again, the leaven is always at work. So long as we claim to be part of Christendom we can never wholly ignore the fact that Christ said, "You know that they which are accounted to rule over the Gentiles lord it over them; but it is not so among you." We tend to take a worldly satisfaction in being called "Doctor, Doctor," but our satisfaction is dimmed when we remember that Jesus said, "Be not called, Rabbi, Rabbi," which means the same thing. The medieval

[5] Acts, 17:26.

world goes in for splendor; but along comes a man like St. Francis, who drinks again of the fountain that is the gospel, and his subsequent life is a tacit criticism of the splendor about him.

In spite of the recurrent failure of the church to be true to Christ's teaching, in this important matter, the fact remains that the gospel continues to this day to be the chief antidote to the cult of power which has been the worst scourge of our distraught century. The real brake on Hitler's doctrines, as on those of Nietzsche before him, is still the gospel of Jesus Christ. If it did nothing else but keep alive in the world the disturbing and revolutionary notion that humble service is better than strutting power, wise men would support and foster the church with all the strength at their command.

After we listen to all the familiar criticisms of the church, including its provincialism, the hypocrisy of its members, the self-centeredness of its leaders, and after we have agreed with all these criticisms, we may still find it reasonable to believe that the church is the only foundation on which our tottering civilization can be restored. It is the stone that our modern builders have rejected, but it may actually be the indispensable cornerstone. We begin to suspect that this is the case when we see the record of the church in the midst of our world storm. The record of the church has not been perfect, but it has been better than its despisers expected. This is conspicuously true in China, where the identification of Christian missionaries with their wounded and broken Chinese friends has made thoughtful men everywhere a bit ashamed of their rather cheap jibes at the missionary enterprise.

All the world knows of the way in which representative members of the Confessional Church of Germany have given the Nazis their toughest opposition. It is part of the record that the labor unions and the universities and learned societies bowed the knee to Baal, when Pastor Niemoeller and his kind stood up like men. The testimony of Albert Einstein in this connection is well known, but it cannot be repeated too often:

Being a lover of freedom, when the revolution came in Germany, I looked to the universities to defend it, knowing that they had always boasted of their devotion to the cause of truth; but, no, the universities immediately were silenced. Then I looked to the great editors of the newspapers whose flaming editorials in days gone by had proclaimed their love of freedom; but they, like the universities, were silenced in a few short weeks. . . .

Only the church stood squarely across the path of Hitler's campaign for suppressing truth. I never had any special interest in the Church before, but now I feel a great affection and admiration because the Church alone has had the courage and persistence to stand for intellectual truth and moral freedom. I am forced thus to confess that what I once despised I now praise unreservedly.[6]

[6] *Time*, December 23, 1940, p. 38.

This is an extremely sobering report, coming as it does from one who has no conceivable private stake in the success of the church. And such a witness does not stand alone. Lewis Mumford, who specifically disclaims being a theologian, has made observations like those made by Einstein and comes to the conclusion that the church is humanity's hope. "And a Church," he writes, "that taught one part of mankind to walk upright and unafraid through one Dark Age may yet summon up the power that will enable us to avert another Dark Age, or to face it, if it begins to descend upon us, with unyielding courage."[7]

At this point the average modern faces a real problem. He may be convinced that individual religion is insufficient, especially in the present storm, either to strengthen the individual or to maintain the testimonies which we prize, but when he proposes to join a church he is baffled. Instead of a church, he finds churches. Shall he join the Roman Catholics, or shall he seek fellowship with one of the many Protestant churches, perhaps the one nearest him or the one where he already has friends? He would like to join the trunk, but he cannot find anything but branches.

There is no doubt that the difficulty is sometimes great, but it is one which the unfriendly critic tends to distort. Sectarianism is often, though not always, an evil. Sometimes a special Christian group keeps

[7] Lewis Mumford, *Faith for Living*, pp. 173, 174.

alive some testimony that might otherwise be lost and all others are consequently indebted to them. In the little churches, so easy to caricature, there are frequently found a genuine sharing of life and a generosity of giving that are sufficient to make the average critic ashamed of his criticism. It is the funny little churches, all over the land, that have provided the money that has made possible the courageous work of the missionaries in China who have, in great numbers, stayed with their Chinese friends in the face of invasion and personal danger or death.

The truth is that a good part of the objection to denominationalism no longer applies to the present situation. The refusal of the Roman Catholics to have any part in the ecumenical movement is a genuine difficulty, but, in spite of this, the amount of agreement among most Christian groups is now very great indeed. The great ecumenical conferences of recent years have shown that most of the denominations have more in common than was generally supposed. We begin to realize that this is the case when we try the experiment of hearing various Christian leaders and guessing what their denominational affiliation is. We have little success. The point is, then, that, though various denominations still exist, it often makes little practical difference which one a man joins since they have so much essential unity.

It may be, however, that some, while convinced of the insufficiency of individual religion, cannot find a church which satisfies them. Since the necessity of social witness remains, anyone in this situation ought to start a church of his own. The imperfection of the present churches does not absolve a man who cares about civilization from seeking to join in the kind of group action that will help to conserve what cannot be conserved by mere individual faith and worship.

Instead of being baffled by any difficulties that we may feel about church membership we need to ask ourselves quite seriously where else we may turn. What organized institution is there, apart from the church, that has as its major purpose the fostering of Justice, Mercy, and Truth and the Freedom that they jointly make possible. Bad and divided as the church may be, it is the only organization really working at the job of affecting men's lives in the deep way in which they must be affected if what we prize is to survive.

It might be supposed that we could turn to the schools, since the task of the schools is constantly being enlarged, but the very nature of the modern school precludes this, as we have already noted in Chapter I.[8] It cannot be the universities, since they touch only a small fraction of the population at best and, furthermore, many universities reject the notion that they are responsible for the spiritual life of their students. There are, of course,

[8] For a careful and scholarly study of this problem see Alvin W. Johnson, *The Legal Status of Church-State Relationships in the United States with Special Reference to the Public Schools*, University of Minnesota Press, 1934.

many different agencies keeping up different phases of what we have defined as the life of the spirit, but they are not sufficient, even when taken all together, for they do not give the dynamic of an organized faith.

If faith is to be effective in undergirding civilized society, it must be given some concrete embodiment. Civilization will not be saved because there are men and women who make the mere affirmation that God exists. Life is not raised to new levels by the mere fact that we have been intellectually convinced by the cosmological argument. Our predicament is too great and too serious for our salvation to come in so academic a manner. What is needed is something that can set men's souls on fire. What is required is a vision of man's life under God's Providence which so thrills us to the center of our beings that we are willing to commit ourselves, soul and body, to the incarnation of that vision.

What, in historical experience, has most often been able to do this? It is that hypocritical, bickering organization that we call the church. Without it we might long ago have been submerged. If our civilization is to be saved, we must have it or something like it, for man is the kind of creature who needs it. The rock on which the church is built often appears to be weather-beaten rubble, because it is all mixed up with human frailty, but the lesson of history is a continual verification of the judgment that the gates of hell cannot prevail against it.

CHAPTER V

The Necessity of a Redemptive Society

~~~~~~~~~~~~~~~~~~~~~~~~~~~~~~~~~~~~~~

There have been high civilizations in the past which have not been Christian, but in the world as we know it I believe that civilization must have a Christian basis and must ultimately rest on the Christian Church.

LORD TWEEDSMUIR

《《《《 》》》》

IT WAS said in Chapter I of this book that the war is not so much the *cause* of the sickness of our civilization as a *symptom* or a *demonstration* of that sickness. We can now go further and say truly that the war is partly a *means of hiding from us the serious character of the sickness*. Since it is relatively easy to unite men *negatively*, i.e., for purposes of combat, we have come to be more optimistic about our culture than conditions warrant. Many of the wounds of our body politic have seemed to be healed during the course of the struggle, everyone being conspicuously patriotic, but actually the wounds are still present and the healing has been only superficial. The worst phenomena of racial hatred, for example, have been merely *postponed*. The new Fascism has not yet been openly espoused.

The most dangerous time that Western civilization has known for many generations is immediately before us. It is the period of convalescence. The threat of world tyranny having been surmounted, there will be a strong temptation to suppose that all is well, but the dangers will actually be far greater than they have already been. All kinds of malignant germs will be offered a splendid opportunity for growth in the post-war world.

Though the war has been carried on so far as a sordid but necessary business, with very little talk about ideals, it remains true that the spirits of many of our soldiers and civilian workers have been supported by the recurring thought of real oppression in the modern world. Eyewitness stories of what has occurred and continues to occur in concentration camps have aroused many of our people to a great desire to set the captives free. This has been combined in varying degrees with the motive of national or cultural survival, the latter motive being especially strong in our country after the attack on Pearl Harbor. Not only in England but in America men have been given abundant reason to believe that they are fighting for their lives and liberties, and the spectacle of conquered countries has given point to this belief. When we have mentioned these two motives, we have said about all there is to say on the subject so far.

The chief point to note about these two motives, the motive of liberation and the motive of survival, is that they can suddenly come to an end, so far as their effectiveness is concerned. When the oppressor is forcibly deprived of his power to oppress, both motives are removed at once. Then the question is: What will hold us together in the Western world? The well-known fact that our young men have performed conspicuous deeds of gallantry against Japanese and Germans is no evidence that we have an adequate spiritual structure for our society when the pressure from Japanese and Germans is removed. Furthermore, one who is at all close to the men in the services cannot be blind to the perplexity of many of the men, even while the fighting continues.

The task, then, is still before us—the task of making a decent world in our modern technical age, *after* the elimination of such open enemies of Christian civilization as Hitler and his kind. *We have argued, in previous chapters, that this cannot be accomplished without ethical convictions, that the ethical convictions cannot be made to prevail if separated from their religious roots, and that the religious roots cannot be nourished apart from the organized church or something like it.* If this reasoning is sound, we are carried forward to a final question concerning the nature of the organized movements without which civilization as we know it will perish. We need to be both precise and concrete in our proposals.

Men are saved by faith, but not by just *any* faith. Though the absence of faith means eventual spiritual death, the presence of faith does not ensure spiritual life, since there are many kinds of faith and there are radically different *objects* of faith. It is true that there can be no thorough regeneration of society except at the religious level, but this does not mean that *any* religion will suffice. There are good religions and there are bad religions and there are many that include some good along with some evil. The logic of events that points to the necessity of a religious reformation of civilization is no evidence of the sufficiency of any particular existent religion or even of all existent religions combined. Civilization may be hopeless on the basis of irreligion, but it may likewise be hopeless on the basis of some of the religions we know.

The church, broadly speaking, has been the chief means by which our most regenerative influences have been preserved, but, even so, we must admit that many of the parts of the church are now in a much-weakened condition. The Confessional Church of Germany has thrilled the world by its courageous stand against tyranny, but there are many churchmen who have, during the same critical period of history, compromised with tyrants. Civilization needs the church, as we argued in Chapter IV, but the church itself needs something to revive it. What do we do when even the salt has lost its savor?

The saving faith we need will not come of itself but must be consciously fostered and spread. It was in this kind of work that Augustine and his associates were so successful in the dark times following the decline of Roman culture. They made a church adequate to the needs of the time, something that could survive even when the empire went to pieces. The close parallel already suggested makes it reasonable to suppose, in advance of specific arguments, that our central need is for a contemporary redemptive society which will do for us what the redemptive society envisaged by Augustine did for his generation and for succeeding generations. Christianity won in the Roman Empire, not chiefly as a belief, though it was a belief, but more as a self-conscious fellowship, and there is nothing in subsequent history to make us suppose that the faith adequate for our day will win in any other way.

In this the children of light may profit by the wisdom of the children of this world, who, as Jesus said, are often wiser in their generation than the children of light are.[1] Perhaps the most original part of *Mein Kampf* and also the part which bears the marks of the greatest intellectual care is that in which Hitler outlines his conception of membership. He distinguishes between "supporters" and

[1] St. Luke, 16:8.

"members." The supporters are the many well-wishers who can be reached rather easily by propaganda and are consequently helpful, but no great new movement could succeed if it merely had supporters. Far more important than the supporters are the actual *members*, the relatively few who can count on one another in every eventuality and who constitute the striking power. It is really better that the number of the members should not be large, since the moment it becomes large it is evident that the strict qualifications for membership have been relaxed.

The idea of membership involves the notion that the nation or the world is the mission field while the party is the missionary band. "The victory of an idea will be possible the sooner," says Hitler, "the more comprehensively propaganda has prepared people as a whole and the more exclusive, rigid, and firm the organization which carries out the fight in practice." Those who are to be influenced, so as to adopt the new thought, cannot, in the nature of things, be too many, but the membership can easily be too large. Accordingly any movement that hopes to be effective must guard against the natural temptation to show early numerical success. "If propaganda has imbued a whole people with an idea, the organization can draw the consequences with a handful of men."

The key to Hitler's idea is the difference between propaganda and organization. "The first task of propaganda is to win people for subsequent organization; the first task of organization is to win men for the continuation of propaganda." The organization is just as crucial as is propaganda, and even more crucial, because the propaganda is wasted without it. Therefore entrance into membership is a serious matter, and, as soon as the movement begins to succeed, enrollment should immediately be blocked and the organization should be allowed to grow only with extreme caution. The following passage is a convenient summary:

In every really great world-shaking movement, propaganda will first have to spread the idea of this movement. Thus it will indefatigably attempt to make the new thought processes clear to the others, and therefore to draw them over to their own ground, or to make them uncertain of their previous conviction. Now, since the dissemination of an idea, that is, propaganda, must have a firm backbone, the doctrine will have to give itself a solid organization. The organization obtains its members from the general body of supporters won by propaganda. The latter will grow the more rapidly, the more intensively the propaganda is carried on, and the latter in turn can work better, the stronger and more powerful the organization is that stands behind it.[2]

We are foolish indeed if we permit our abhorrence of Hitler, both in his methods and his aims, to blind us to the practical wisdom that these quotations express. Hitler has demonstrated the wisdom

[2] These quotations from *Mein Kampf* are from the new Houghton Mifflin edition, Boston, 1943, pp. 582-584.

of the indicated procedure by employing it with remarkable success in the service of a bad cause. There is no reason why it cannot be employed in a good cause. Hitler has spoken much that is false, but he was not speaking falsely when he said, *"All great movements, whether of a religious or a political nature, must attribute their mighty successes only to the recognition and application of these principles, and all lasting successes in particular are not even thinkable without consideration of these laws."*[3]

When we begin to apply these principles to the task before all men of good will, we get something like the following: We need a world-shaking movement to offset the planetary dangers that a peculiar combination of factors has now produced. What is required to save us from the destruction of which world wars constitute a foretaste is a new spirit. We need this far more desperately than we need any new machine or anything else. We are fairly clear concerning the nature of this new spirit, since it has been tested repeatedly in the religious tradition out of which our highest moral standards have come, even though it is now so largely ignored. We must spread this spirit by the written and spoken word, as many are already doing, though nowhere in sufficient force. But we must go beyond this to the formation of cells, made up of men and women who are as single-minded in their devotion to the redemptive task as the early

[3] *Ibid.*, pp. 585, 586.

Nazi party members were to the task of National Socialism.

The kind of organized movement that the need of the hour suggests does not at present exist. Certainly the existent church cannot function in this way because *Christianity has long ceased to be scrupulous in membership.* Some may be members because they are greatly concerned over the redemption of our civilization, but they are surrounded by millions who are members because they were born that way or because membership helps their social standing. Since the devoted and effective group cannot be *found*, it must be *made*.

The present is the time for some creative and urgent dreaming about the nature of the redemptive society that is so clearly necessary. This society may be as different from the conventional church of today as an airplane is different from a buggy. But just as a buggy and an airplane have the same fundamental purpose, namely, transportation, so the church of today and the religious society of tomorrow may have the same redemptive purpose, though new problems require new vision.

Our time is not unique in the need of new movements that can bring spiritual refreshment, since the process has been illustrated repeatedly in crucial times. We need only to remind ourselves of the immense importance of the Franciscan movement, of the Society of Jesus, of the Children of the Light, as the associates of George Fox were called in the seventeenth century, of the new fellowships inspired and organized by the Wesleys.

The sad truth is that such unconventional religious movements, after being wonderfully salutary at the beginning, tend to become conventional until finally they take their place among those which require revivication. The Children of the Light did marvelous things in the seventeenth century; for a while, it looked as though the Quaker movement might be a renewing power in the whole culture of Christendom, but soon Quakers allowed themselves to become a mere sect, one church among others. Then they were merely a competing organization and no longer an activating force in the entire culture.

Now it is again necessary to create and organize a radically new kind of society engaged in a perennially necessary task. It is not within the scope of this book to engage in the question of what the precise nature of such a society must be. Such a discussion would obscure the outline of the logical structure that it is our purpose to present. But we may point out briefly that the specific character of the redemptive society is of crucial importance. For example, the redemptive society must be unconventional, but mere unconventionality is not enough. We have lately seen, in the experience of the Oxford Groups, a demonstration of the way in which a new and unconventional religious fellowship may fail of the highest purpose because of insufficiently rigorous thought.

The mistakes of the Oxford Groups and the consequent ill repute of their movement should make us realize how carefully we must think through the problem before us; but, at the same time, the relative success of this movement should open our eyes to the power that lies in really devoted groups. The same lesson can be learned from numerous cults, of which Jehovah's Witnesses constitute one of the most striking examples. The path of wisdom lies not in rejecting a method, in itself successful, because it has had associated with it some unpleasant features. The path of wisdom lies rather in seeing how the successful method can be retained and employed while the unpleasant features are detached from it.

The idea that salvation, both for individuals and society, comes through the work of living fellowships is as old as Christianity and older. We have said that it is incumbent upon the children of light to borrow the wisdom of the children of this world, but the earlier borrowing was the other way around, inasmuch as the technic which Hitler so carefully describes is essentially the technic of the first Christian victory. John the Baptist was a voice crying in the wilderness, but Jesus was not, because he depended on the way in which twelve men were bound together. The fellowship of the

Nazi party members is a kind of parody of the *Koinonia*.

It is interesting to note that when Hitler wants to express the kind of relation which must exist among the individuals who make up an effective central organization, and when he wants a strong word to contrast with mere "supporters," he is forced to rely on specifically Christian terminology and speak of "members." Apparently nobody ever spoke of being a member of anything until the term was coined to express the relationship that existed, at least ideally, among the first Christians. In the beginning, when St. Paul first used it, the figure of speech must have seemed extreme or even grotesque. He said Christians had the relation to one another that exists between the parts of a body. As though the original figure were not strong enough, St. Paul went on to speak of a situation in which men are "members one of another."[4]

Here lies a path of redemption for which many in the modern world are waiting, even though they do not realize what it is they seek. There is a vast amount of loneliness, and a consequent desire to belong to something. This is shown by the success of new cults and by the emergence of groups in which fellowship is genuine, even though, as judged by conventional standards, hardly respectable. For example, the organization called Alcoholics Anonymous appears to have an enormous influence in

[4] Ephesians, 4:25 and Romans, 12:5. See also I. Corinthians, 12.

the lives of its members. Its paradoxical entrance qualifications sound peculiarly Christian, in that each man must admit that he is too weak to help himself and that each undertakes to help another.

Real fellowship is so rare and so precious that it is like dynamite in any human situation. Any group that will find a way to the actual sharing of human lives will make a difference either for good or ill in the modern world or in any world. But fellowship is always more likely to be genuine if men are united *for* something. The problem of purpose, however, really solves itself, so far as the present discussion is concerned. Those who see the danger in which our civilization lies and who have some intimation of the spiritual renewal without which our present order cannot possibly be saved have a ready-made purpose to draw them together. What we want is a group so devoted to this purpose and so tightly organized that it can work as effectively for redemptive ends in our time as the first Christians worked for redemptive ends in the first century of our era and as the Nazis have worked for divisive ends in the first century of their would-be era.

The way to begin is to take seriously Hitler's principle of limitation of membership. Consider, for example, a university campus as a field of missionary labor. A group of fifty really devoted Christians who are not in the least apologetic and who are willing to make the spread of the gospel their first interest would affect mightily any campus in the country, no matter how great the initial opposition might be. The same can be said of an average town. The prospects for the gospel might be better if the average town had only a few dozen Christians in place of the few thousand church members now listed.

It is not necessary, in our spiritual enterprise, to lay the arbitrary limitation on numbers that Hitler undertook in forming the Nazi party, since the limitation appears in the nature of the situation. There are not actually too many potential members anywhere. The problem is to *find* them, to unite them, and to make them into an effective organization cutting across all existent barriers.

One of the greatest weaknesses of the churches as now organized is not merely that they include so many who are irreligious, but that they fail to include so many who are deeply religious, though they may not express their religion in traditional ways. Many of those who believe most strongly that there is no redemption of civilization apart from religion are not in the church, with the consequent loss both to themselves and to the organized religious forces. Characteristic men in this situation are Walter Lippmann and Lewis Mumford. It is easy to quote passages from the work of both these thinkers to show how much concerned they are over the religious life of the Western world. In his *Good Society*, Walter Lippmann reserves his religious discussion for the climax of his book, in which he shows why tyranny finds its mortal enemy in religion:

By the religious experience the humblest communicant is led into the presence of a power so much greater than his master's that the distinctions of this world are of little importance. So it is no accident that the only open challenge to the totalitarian state has come from men of deep religious faith. For in their faith they are vindicated as immortal souls, and from this enhancement of their dignity they find the reason why they must offer a perpetual challenge to the dominion of men over men.[5]

In similar vein Lewis Mumford has made an unambiguous testimony: "The crisis, then, presses toward a conversion, deep-seated, organic, religious in essence, so that no part of political or personal existence will be untouched by it."[6]

The redemptive society we seek must include men such as these and not merely those who have been identified with ecclesiastical enterprises. Many of the best people are not in the church precisely because they *are* the best people. We have, of course, some conspicuously vigorous minds actively at work within the church and wholly devoted to it, William Temple, T. S. Eliot and Reinhold Niebuhr being striking illustrations of this; but too many of essentially similar spirit are outside

[5] Walter Lippmann, *The Good Society*, Little, Brown & Company, Boston, 1937, p. 382.

[6] Lewis Mumford, *Faith for Living*, Harcourt, Brace and Company, New York, 1940, pp. 193, 196.

any self-conscious religious organization. Consequently the lines must be redrawn. "No religion," writes T. S. Eliot in his famous essay on Lancelot Andrewes, "can survive the judgment of history unless the best minds of its time have collaborated in its construction."[7]

The church of Elizabeth's time, Eliot argues, succeeded because it had the advantage of the collaboration of men of the intellectual stature of Hooker and Andrewes. But on what do the intellectual giants of our day collaborate? They collaborate on economic planning, they collaborate on foreign policy, they collaborate on military strategy, but on the matters of the greatest possible importance and urgency they do not collaborate. Relatively few give themselves loyally to a consciously contrived fellowship of work and worship. Consequently the representative men of our day are closer to the tradition of John the Baptist than to the tradition of Christ. They are indeed voices crying in the wilderness. Many speak truly and well, but they are not members one of another and their influence is dissipated because they are not joined together in a redemptive society. Unless this situation is altered, there is little hope for our civilization.

Pessimistic as the more thoughtful spokesmen of this generation necessarily are, it would not be

[7] T. S. Eliot, *Essays Ancient and Modern*, Harcourt, Brace and Company, New York, 1936, p. 7.

fair to bring this sense of the meeting to a close without reference to the deep faith that underlies so much of the intellectual and spiritual searching of our time. We have to strive to keep our faith, but we *are* keeping it. We are perplexed, but not unto despair. We believe that we can survive a civilization gone rotten and that the essential faith of Western man can be restored to this end. The moral decay of imperial Rome was overcome by the gospel for that day, and the moral decay of Western civilization will be likewise overcome by the gospel for our day. If modern man can be made to see and understand the predicament he is in, that very recognition may be amazingly salutary. As a fitting conclusion to this book, nothing better could be found than some sentences that Lord Tweedsmuir wrote just before he died, words that seem to the author to be the true conclusion of the matter. "I believe—and this is my crowning optimism—that the challenge with which we are now faced may restore to us that manly humility which alone gives power. It may bring us back to God. In that case our victory is assured. The Faith is an anvil which has worn out many hammers."